earthen **lamps**

T0125050

OSHO

Stories and parables written by Osho

earthen **lamps**

60 Parables and Anecdotes to Light Up Your Heart

ABOUT OUR MORTAL BODY OF CLAY AND THE IMMORTAL FLAME OF CONSCIOUSNESS

OSHO

Originally published in Hindi as *Mitti Ke Diye*, by Osho. The complete OSHO text archive can be found via the online OSHO Library at www.osho.com/Library

OSHO is a registered trademark of OSHO International Foundation
www.osho.com/trademarks

OSHO MEDIA INTERNATIONAL
New York • Zurich • Mumbai
an imprint of
OSHO INTERNATIONAL
www.osho.com/oshointernational

Distributed by Publishers Group Worldwide
www.pgw.com

Library of Congress Catalog-In-Publication Data is available

Printed in India by Manipal Technologies Limited, Karnataka

ISBN 978-1-938755-87-3
This title is also available in eBook format ISBN 978-0-88050-075-3

Contents

Introduction

Introduction by Osho

W hat do I find when I look deeply into man? I find that man, too, is an earthen lamp! But he is not just a lamp made of clay; in him there is also a flame of light that is constantly rising towards the sun. Only his body is made of earth, his soul is that very flame. But whoever forgets this continuously rising flame of light remains just clay. He stops rising upwards. And when there is no rising upwards there is no life.

My friend, look within. Get rid of all the smoke in your mind and see this flame of consciousness. Raise your vision beyond that which is mortal in you, and recognize the immortal. There is nothing more precious than recognizing this, because with this recognition the animal in you will die and godliness will be born.

Preface

A parable is a way of saying things in an indirect way. Truth cannot be asserted directly. That is too violent, too aggressive, too male. Truth can only be said in a very indirect way. It can be hinted at, indicated. You cannot be convinced of the truth: you can only be persuaded.

And the master is one who is not going to convince you of the truth but who is going to seduce you into truth. Parables are very seductive. Even those who were not searching for any truth may be suddenly struck by a parable: something may become suddenly available to them.

People like stories. And the stories have a tendency to hang around your consciousness. It is difficult to forget them; it is very easy to remember them. They have a way of reaching to the deepest core of your being.

Osho
The Perfect Master, Vol. 1

The Music of the Sea 1

I have heard a story:

Thousands of years ago, a town which had many temples dedicated to the gods was drowned beneath the sea.

The bells of those drowned temples are still ringing. It may be that the tidal waters make them ring, or maybe they keep ringing because the fish strike them as they swim here and there. But whatever the reason is, the bells are still ringing even today, and even today, their sweet music can be heard from the seashore.

I also wanted to hear this music, so I went in search of that beach. After several years of wandering, I finally found it. But all I could hear was the loud tumult of the sea. The sound of the waves crashing on the rocks resounded again and again in that lonely place, but there was no music nor were the temple bells ringing. I kept listening intently but on the shore nothing could be heard except the sound of the breaking waves.

Even so I waited there. In fact, I had forgotten the way back and now that unknown, lonely seashore seemed destined to witness the end of my life. And by and by, even the thought of listening to the bells disappeared. I settled down on the beach.

Then one night, I suddenly heard the bells of those underwater temples ringing, and their sweet music began to fill my life with joy.

On hearing the music I awoke from my sleep, and since then I have not been able to sleep again. Now someone is constantly awake within me, sleep has vanished forever, and my life has been filled with light – because where there is no sleep, there is no darkness.

And I am happy. In fact, I have become happiness incarnate, because how can sadness exist when music from God's temple can be heard?

Do you also want to go to that seashore? Do you also want to hear the music of those underwater temples? Then let us go, let us move within ourselves. The heart is the sea, and in its depth is found the city with the underwater temples.

But only those who are, in every way, calm and alert will be able to hear the music of those temples. How can this music be heard when there are the loud conflicts of thought and desire? Even the desire to hear this music becomes an obstacle to discovering it.

Life Is as We Make It 2

One dark night, I was looking at the stars in the sky. The whole town was asleep and I was feeling very compassionate towards those sleeping souls: after a day's hard work, those poor fellows must have been dreaming about the fulfillment of their unfulfilled desires. In dreams they were living and in dreams they slept. They saw neither the sun nor the moon nor the stars. In fact, the eyes that see dreams cannot see that which is really there. It is absolutely essential for the dust of dreams to disappear before the truth can be seen.

As the darkness of night deepened, the number of stars in the sky increased. Gradually, the whole sky was full of their shimmering light. And not only the sky – I too was filled with their silent beauty.

Isn't the sky of the soul filled with stars when it sees them in the sky? The truth is that man gets filled with what he sees. The person who sees the small, is filled with the small; the one who sees the great, is filled with that greatness. Our eyes are the gateways to our souls.

Sitting against a tree, I was simply lost in the sky when from behind me someone placed his cold, dead hand on my shoulder. I could also hear the sound of his feet. They were not the sounds of a living being, and his hand was so lifeless that even in the darkness it took me no time to understand the thoughts behind his eyes. This contact with his body had brought even the winds of his mind to me. That person was living, he was young, but life had left him long ago, and youth had perhaps never come his way.

We both sat down under the stars. I took his lifeless hands into my own so that they could become slightly warmer and the heat of my life might also flow into his. He was alone but maybe love could bring him back to life.

Without a doubt, it was not the moment to speak, and so I kept silent. Sometimes the heart finds closeness in silence, and wounds which words cannot fill are healed – silence can heal them too. Words and sounds are a disturbance and an obstacle to understanding the whole music.

The night was peaceful and still. The silent music caught hold of us both. He was no longer unfamiliar to me; I was there, in him. Then his stone-like stillness ended and his tears told me that he was melting. He was weeping, his entire body was trembling. The currents of what was weeping in his heart were touching every sinew of his body. He kept weeping, weeping, weeping, and then he said, "I want to die. I am extremely poor and disappointed. I have absolutely nothing."

I remained silent some time and then slowly told him I was reminded of a story…

A young man told a mystic, "Existence has taken everything away from me. I have no choice but death."

I asked him if he was not that same young man.

The mystic told the young man, "I see a big treasure hidden within you. Will you sell it? If you sell it, you will gain everything and will also save existence from being given a bad name."

Again I asked him if he wasn't that same young man. I could not say for sure, but I was that very mystic and it seemed as if the story was repeating itself.

The young man in the story was surprised.

And maybe the young man I was talking to was also becoming surprised.

He said, "Treasure? I don't even have a penny to my name."

Then the mystic started laughing and said, "Come. Let us go to the king. The king is very clever. He always keeps a keen eye out for hidden treasure. He will definitely purchase your treasure. In the past I have taken many sellers of hidden treasures to him."

The young man could not understand. For him everything the mystic was saying was a puzzle. But nevertheless he set off with him towards the king's palace.

On the way, the mystic told him, "There are a few things which should be settled in advance so that there will be no quarrel before the king. This king is someone who will refuse nothing if he likes it, whatever the cost. Therefore, it is important to know whether you are ready to sell these things or not?"

That young man said, "What treasure? What things?"

The mystic said, "For instance, your eyes? What will you charge for them? I can get you up to fifty thousand rupees for them from the king. Is that enough? Or your heart and mind? For them you can get up to a hundred thousand rupees each."

The young man was surprised; he felt that the mystic was crazy. He asked, "Have you gone mad? Eyes? Heart? Mind? What is all this you are talking about? I cannot sell them for any price. And not just me – nobody can sell them."

The mystic started laughing and said, "Have I gone mad or have you? When you have so many valuable things which you cannot sell even for hundreds of thousands of rupees, why do you pretend to be poor? Use them. The treasure trove which is not used is empty even when it is full, and the treasure trove that is used is full even when it is empty. Existence gives us treasures, immense treasures, but one has to search and dig for them by oneself. There is no wealth bigger than life itself and one who cannot even see wealth in that will not find it anywhere else."

It was past midnight. I got up and I said to the young man, "Go, go to sleep, and tomorrow wake up a different man. Life is what we make it. It is our own creation. We can make it something dead, or we can make it eternal – as we choose. And this depends on no one else except our own selves. And death will follow by itself; there is no need to invite it."

Invite life. Invite enlightenment. That you can gain only through hard work, effort, resolve and constant application.

Giving Up Renunciation 3

A king was very famous. The news of his charity had spread far and wide. His humility, self-denial, his simple living and purity were praised by everyone, and the result was that his ego knew no bounds. He was as far away from godliness as a man could be.

How easy it is to rise in the eyes of man, but how difficult it is to be close to existence! And one who desires to rise in the eyes of men, invariably falls down in the eyes of existence, because he is just the opposite on the inside to what he appears to be on the outside. Because the physical eyes of man cannot penetrate so deeply a person can easily fall into self-deception.

But surely a person's own insight can reach to that depth? In the end, there is no value in the image he creates of himself for the eyes of other men. What *is* valuable is the image that unfolds before his own inner eyes. That same image, his utter nakedness is also reflected in the mirror of existence. In the end what a person sees of himself is the same as what stands before existence.

The king's fame continued to rise, but his soul was drowning. His fame continued to spread while his soul kept shrinking. His branches were spreading but his roots were growing weak.

He had a friend. That friend was the Kubera, the lord of riches, in those days. Just as the rivers and tributaries all meet in the ocean, so streams of wealth met in his treasure chest. He was entirely different from his friend, the king. He would not part with a penny in the name of charity. He was infamous.

The king and the rich man both became old. One was filled with ego, the other with remorse. Pride gave one of them pleasure and remorse pricked the other one's soul. As death approached, the king held more and more tightly onto his ego. It was something to hold on to. But at last the rich man's remorse became a revolution inside him. *His* ego could no longer be his support. It became necessary to give it up.

But let us remember that remorse is the other side of pride, and so it is also very difficult to leave behind. Very often when remorse is turned upside-down, it becomes pride. For this same reason pleasure-seekers become saints, the greedy become charitable, and the cruel full of pity. But basically there is no revolution in their souls.

That rich man went to a master. He said to him, "I am perturbed. I am burning up in a fire. I want peace."

The master asked, "Could you not find peace with so much wealth, fame, power and ability?"

He said, "No. I have fully realized that there is no peace in wealth."

The master then said, "So go and give back everything that you have to those from whom you snatched it away. Then come back to me. Come back to me after you have become simple and poor."

The rich man did so. When he came back the master asked, "What now?"

He said, "Now I have no support except you."

But that master was very strange; we might say that he was mad. He turned that poor rich man out of his hut and closed his doors. The night was dark and the forest was lonely. There was no other shelter in the forest except that hut.

The rich man thought that he was returning after doing something great, but what was this welcome, what was this reception he had received?

He had discovered that the accumulation of wealth was useless, but that the renunciation of wealth was also a waste!

That night he slept under a tree with no support. Now he was unsupported, with no friends and no home. He had neither wealth nor power, neither possessions nor renunciation. But when he woke up in the morning he found that he was immersed in a peace which cannot be described in words. A mind which has no support finds the support of existence without any difficulty.

He ran to fall at the master's feet, but instead he found the master falling down at his feet. The master embraced him and said, "It is easier to give up wealth but more difficult to give up renunciation. But only the one who can give up renunciation can really give up wealth. It is easy to renounce the world but more difficult to give up a master. But he who can also give up a master can find the great master. Whether it is the support of wealth or of renunciation, of remorse or of pride, of the world or of saintliness – in fact whatever the support is – it will be an obstruction on the way to godliness.

"As soon as the other supports fall away, the supreme support is found. Whether I look for support from wealth or religion, as long as I am searching for support, I am only searching to protect my ego. As soon as I give up that support, as soon as I am unsupported and unprotected, the mind becomes submerged in the basic existence of the self. That is peace, that is salvation, that is nirvana. Do you want to discover anything else?"

The man – who by now was now neither a master of wealth nor of poverty – said, "No. The very thought of possessing was a mistake. I was lost precisely because of that. Whatever needed to be found has already been found. It was only in the race to possess that I lost that which is never lost and forever found. Now I want neither peace nor even nirvana. I am not, and what exists is peace, godliness, and salvation."

What Is a Religious Mind? 4

I was sitting among a group of old men. They had all retired and were talking intently with one another, but to no avail, about this world and the next. They would have said they were discussing religion.

In a way this was true, because what we call the scriptures are also full of this same kind of worthless gossip. Sometimes I get the feeling that maybe the so-called scriptures were created by these very same old men.

If religion is anything, it is life itself. But what connection does this have with useless theories? If religion is anything, it is our discovery of our true selves. But what connection does this have with useless gossip?

But the scriptures are all full of words, and the minds of the so-called religious people keep scrambling up into the skies with their dreams. The scriptures and their teachings do not allow true religion a passage of entry into their minds.

What is a religious mind?

My definition of a religious mind is a mind free from all kinds of words, teachings, and thoughts. A religious mind is not an imaginative mind. On the contrary, there is no other kind of understanding that is more mundane and that stands on the solid base of truth.

While I was enjoying listening to the old men's conversation, a saint came by. At that moment they were discussing how man gains salvation: through what kinds of efforts, and how many lives it takes. The saint also jumped into this discussion – without a doubt he had a greater right to an opinion and therefore his voice was the loudest.

Each person found support from the scriptures for their opinion, but nobody was prepared to listen to or accept the views of anyone else. One old man was of the opinion that salvation is gained only after doing severe penance over hundreds of lives. Another thought that this was not at all necessary as deliverance comes solely through the grace of God. A third one said that since our state of unworthiness is an illusion, the question of overcoming unworthiness through penance does not arise: with one glimpse of true understanding it simply disappears, just like the imagined snake that we see in a rope.

Then someone asked me, "What do you think?

What could I say? I had been hiding myself in a corner in case somebody's eyes caught mine. I had no knowledge of the scriptures since, luckily, I had not made the mistake of going down that road. Therefore, even when asked, I kept quiet. But, soon after, someone asked me again, "Why don't you say something?" Even if I had wanted to say something, what could I say? While so many of them were speaking, I was the only one listening. Even then I still kept quiet. Perhaps my very silence started speaking; because eventually the attention of all of them was focused on me. Perhaps they were all tired and wanted a rest.

I was caught and I had to say something. So I told them a story:

In a certain village there was a custom that whenever a young man was married, either he or his family had to spend at least five thousand rupees on the marriage ceremony. The village was very rich and no marriages were performed there for less. This was even written down in the village scriptures. Nobody had read those scriptures, but this was what the priest of that village had told them. And who could question the priest? The scriptures had been written in some local dialect from the past and he had remembered every bit by rote – and scriptures have always been undeniable and unquestionable. What is in them is the truth. What higher authority of truth can there be? If something is in the scriptures then that is a guarantee of its truth.

But on one occasion it happened that a young man and his bride performed their marriage for only five hundred rupees. For sure, this young man must have been a revolutionary, otherwise how could he have done this? The villagers asked him, "How many rupees did you spend?"

He replied, "Five hundred."

Then the village *panchayat*, the group of elders, was summoned and he was told: "This is entirely wrong; a marriage cannot be performed without spending five thousand rupees."

The young man laughed at them and said, "Whether a marriage can or cannot be performed with five hundred rupees means nothing to me. You can keep discussing this. I have got my bride and I am blissful."

After saying this, the young man went back to his house.

I also got up and said to those old men, "Goodbye, my friends. Carry on with your discussions. I will make a move now."

5   Fear Has No Temples

Man is totally alone, he is in darkness. He is without support; he feels unsafe and afraid. This aloneness is his anxiety.

The way to get rid of this fear is religion. Religion is basically the process of becoming fearless. But the religions – "religions" only in name – are very afraid of fearlessness. Their support and very existence depend upon there being fear in the hearts of men. Fear itself is their very nourishment and lifeblood. A climate of fearlessness would herald the end of their lives and livelihoods.

Man's fear has been exploited a great deal. Religions have not lagged behind in this exploitation; perhaps they have even been at the very forefront of it. It is with the support of fear that supernatural beings can exist and with the support of fear that the gods of the religions exist. Superstitions and frightening supernatural beings have merely threatened man – but this has never been more than a lighthearted game. But a "God" who is based on fear has killed man outright; this game has been very costly.

Life has become entangled in webs of fear. How can there be bliss when there is fear, and only more fear? How can there be love? How can there be peace? How can there be truth? Bliss is the outcome of fearlessness. Fear is death; fearlessness is eternal life.

That superstitions thrive on our fear is understandable, but that God should also live off fear is all wrong. And if God is based on fear, then there will be no way for people to get out of the clutches of these superstitions.

I say that God, godliness, has nothing to do with fear. Certainly, under the cover of God someone else is exploiting this fear. Religion is not in the hands of religious people. It is said that whenever truth is discovered, Satan is the first to get hold of it. The people who present and organize religion are not only opposed to it but also fundamentally opposed to one another. Religion has always been in the hands of its enemies, and if this fact is not recognized while there is still time, the future of mankind will not be good or anything worth looking forward to.

Religion has to be saved not from irreligious people, but from the so-called religious ones. And without a doubt, this is a more difficult and troublesome task.

As long as religion is based upon fear, it cannot be real religion. The basis of godliness is love; it has nothing to do with fear. Man needs the god of love; there is no other path to godliness except through love. Fear is not only wrong, but it is also a killer – because where there is fear, there is hatred, and therefore where there is fear, love is not possible.

Religion has thrived on fear and in this way its temples have slowly been destroyed. Temples are for love; temples of fear cannot exist. Fear has no temples; it has only prisons.

I ask you: are the religious temples, temples or prisons? If religion is based on fear, then the temples will be prisons. If religion is based on fear, God himself cannot be anything more than the chief prison officer.

What is religion? Is it a fear of sin, of punishment, of hell? Or is it greed – doing good deeds for the rewards of heaven? No. Religion is neither fear nor greed. Greed is simply an extension of fear. Religion is fearlessness. Religion is freedom from all fears.

Something happened long ago…

Two brothers were living in a town. They were the wealthiest people in that town. Perhaps the name of that town was the "The Town of Darkness."

The elder brother was very religious. Regularly, every day, he would go to the temple. He would give to charities and do good deeds. He would listen to religious discourses and discussions. He would sit in the company of respectable people and saints. Because of him there was a daily gathering of saints in his house.

Because of the attention he paid to God and the saints, he understood that he had become entitled to go to heaven in the next life. The good men and the saints had explained to him that this was confirmed by the scriptures – scriptures that had been compiled by good men and saints just like them. On the one hand, he exploited others and so gained his wealth, and on the other hand he gave to charities and did good works.

Heaven cannot be attained without charities. There is no wealth without exploitation. Wealth is derived from the opposite of religiousness and the religions rely on wealth. He exploited others, and the respectable men and the saints exploited him. Exploiters have always been good friends with one another.

But the older brother had always pitied his younger brother who was no good at accumulating money and, consequently, had become incapable of accumulating religion either. His behavior, full of love and truth, was getting in the way of reaching God. He neither went to the temple nor did he know the *ABC* of the scriptures. His situation was certainly pitiable, and his bank balance in the other world was empty.

The younger brother used to avoid the respectable men and saints, just as others may try to avoid an infectious disease. If the saints entered the house through one door, he would leave from another. His religious brother often used to ask the saints to bring a change of heart to his irreligious brother. But such a change could only happen if he would remain in their presence, and this he would not do.

However, one day a full-fledged, so-called saint arrived at the house. No one knew how many irreligious people he had converted. He was well-versed in the theories of peace, persuasion, threat, and division. It was his whole profession to convert people to religion.

The foundations of religions have rested on such saints. Otherwise, religions would have disappeared long ago.

When the elder brother repeated his request for help to this saint, the saint replied, "Don't worry. That fool will now find himself in trouble. I will immediately make sure that he remembers God. And what I say, I always do."

So saying, he picked up his stick and accompanied the elder brother. He had been a wrestler in the past, but then, finding saintliness a better profession than wrestling, had become a saint. As soon as they went in, he caught hold of the younger brother. Not only did he catch hold of him, but he also knocked him to the ground and sat on his chest. The young man could not understand what was going on, but although he was almost speechless with surprise he managed to ask, "Sir, what is happening?"

The saint replied, "A change of heart!"

The young man laughed and said, "Please get off me. Is this the way to change someone's heart? Please take care; you may hurt me."

The saint said, "We do not believe in the body; we believe in God. Just say 'Ram' and I will leave you alone. Otherwise, you will discover there is no one worse than me."

The saint was a very generous man and so, in the young man's interest, he descended to the level of beating him.

The young man said, "What is the relationship between fear and God? And does God have a name? I will not say 'Ram' when I am in this situation, whether I live or not!" And then he pushed the saint off him.

As he fell the saint cried, "Wonderful, Wonderful! You have said what you had to say! Even in saying 'I will not say "Ram"' you have uttered his name."

The older brother was very angry with his brother because he had pushed the saint over, but he was absolutely delighted with the saint. He had made his atheist brother utter the name of God. The glory of the name of Ram is so great that uttering his name, even by mistake, will take a person beyond the ocean of this life. That day he organized a feast for the whole town. After all, his younger brother had become religious!

The Language of the Devil   6

The worshippers of one god had broken the idols of another god. In fact, this is nothing new. It is always happening. Not only do men rival one another, even their gods are rivals. In fact, the gods they create cannot be very different from them. One temple is opposed to another because one man is opposed to another. One scripture is the enemy of another because one man is the enemy of another.

Man is just like his religion; his situation is the same as that of his gods. Instead of fostering friendship, religions have become the instruments of rivalries, and instead of filling the world with love, they have filled it with the poison of enmity and discord.

I had just returned and had just heard the news about the breaking of these idols, when some of those whose idols had been broken came to see me. They were full of righteous anger. Although no anger can be good, even so, they said that their anger was justified and that they would not rest until they had destroyed their opponents' temples. It was a question of "saving their religion."

When I started laughing, they were surprised. Surely, this was not the time to laugh? They were extremely serious and from their perspective what could be more serious than this threat to their religion?

I asked these friends, "Do you understand the language of the Devil?"

One of them asked, "What language is that?"

They understood the language of the scriptures but not that of the Devil – even though without an understanding of the language of the Devil the scriptures themselves become his scriptures.

I told them a story…

A boat was traveling to a distant land. Among those on board sat a poor monk. Some mischievous people were teasing him in all kinds of ways. While he was praying at night, they thought that he would be unable to protect himself and so they started beating on his head with their shoes. He was deep in prayer and tears of love were falling from his eyes.

Then a voice came from the sky: "My beloved one, you just have to ask and I will overturn the boat."

The antagonists became nervous and the other travelers were also concerned. Their sport was becoming too dangerous. They fell at the monk's feet and started apologizing to him.

When the monk's prayers came to an end he got up and spoke to them saying, "Don't be worried." Then he lifted his face up to the sky and said, "Dear God, in what Devil's language were you talking? If you want to play the game of overturning, overturn the understanding of these people. What is the use in overturning the boat?"

Again, a voice came from the sky, saying: "I am very pleased. You have recognized rightly. The earlier voice was not mine. Only he who can recognize the voice of the Devil can recognize my voice too."

Courage   7

What is the most essential factor in the search for truth?

I say courage: the courage to discover one's authentic self. To know oneself as one is, is the most essential thing. It is very difficult, but without it there can be no understanding of the truth.

What greater hardship is there than coming to know oneself, without any veil, in utter nakedness? But this is the price one has to pay to attain to truth. Only from there does the longing for truth begin in man.

Being true to the self is in itself a manifestation of an intense thirst for truth. How can one who ties himself to the shore of falsehood row his boat across the sea of truth? The shore of falsehood will have to be left behind. That very shore is an obstacle in the journey towards truth. That very shore is the bondage. True, there is safety on that shore and it is that desire for safety which is the stronghold of falsehood.

In our journey towards truth there should be no love of safety. Furthermore, there must be the unshakeable courage to venture out into the unknown. He who does not possess the courage to be unsafe cannot discover the unknown. Without accepting the challenge of being unsafe, no one can throw off his false masks and disguises, nor can he be free from the convictions that he has adopted for safety's sake.

Is it not for the sake of safety that we present ourselves not as we are?

Aren't all these deceptions merely our strategies for feeling safe? And what of our civilizations and cultures? The proud person appears humble, the greedy one dresses up like a renunciate, the exploiter indulges in charity, the killer promotes the rhetoric of peace, and minds filled with hatred speak the language of love.

This self-deception is very easy. When has acting in dramas ever been difficult? In the marketplace of sophistication, attractive toys have always been sold at bargain rates. But remember: a bargain, which on the face of it seems cheap, proves very costly in the long run, because he who hides himself behind such toys gets further and further away from reality. An unbridgeable gulf is created between reality and the person, because his identity is always afraid of losing its cover. He goes on and on hiding himself beneath more and more covers and masks.

Falsehood does not come alone; it is flanked by its armies which come to protect it. Such is the web of self-deception and fear that surrounds us that it becomes impossible to lift our eyes to that which is beyond us. And how can a person who suffers from the fear of losing his particular false mask gather enough strength to uncover the truth? Such strength is found only through having the courage to discard these self-deceptions. A fearful mind is the enemy of seeing the truth.

Who then is the real friend in this situation? Fearlessness is the friend, and fearlessness of mind is gained only by one who can lay bare the truth about himself and can therefore become free from fear. If you continually mask the truth about yourself, fear keeps increasing and the inner being becomes powerless. But if you uncover yourself and look, then fear is drowned in the light of that understanding and you discover new and different sources of energy.

It is this that I call courage: the power to uncover the self and to acknowledge it. This is courage – and it is unavoidable in the attainment of truth. This is the first step towards godliness.

There is a very interesting story…

A young man reached the dwelling of the Rishi Haridrumat Gautam. He wanted to know the truth. He had a desire to know the *brahman*, the ultimate. He placed his head at the feet of the *rishi* and said, "Oh master, I have come in search of truth. Be generous to me and teach me the knowledge of *brahman*; I am blind and I want light."

The name of that young man was Satyakama.

The *rishi* asked him, "My son, what is your lineage? Who is your father? What is his name?"

This young man had no knowledge of his father, nor did he know his lineage.

He went to his mother, asked her, and then returned. He repeated to the *rishi* what his mother had told him.

He said, "Oh master, I do not know my lineage. Nor do I know my father. My mother also does not know who my father is. When I asked her, she said that in her youth she was associating with many respectable people and used to do whatsoever pleased them. She does not know from whom I have descended. The name of my mother is Jabali. Therefore I am Satyakama Jabal. This is what she has asked me to tell you."

Haridrumat was very much moved by the simple truthfulness of the story. He embraced the young man and said, "My dear son, you are definitely a brahmin. So much trust in the truth is the very essence of a brahmin. You will also certainly be able to discover *brahman*, because the truth will come knocking at the doors of one who has the courage to face the truth about himself."

8   Ambition and Inferiority

I call the wheel of life – going round and around on the axle of ambition – hell. It is this fever of ambition that poisons life. Among the most serious diseases and mental troubles that man has known, there is no greater disease than ambition – because a mind which is disturbed by the winds of ambition is not destined to have peace, music, and bliss. Such a person is not at home in himself – and peace, music, and bliss are the outcome of being at home in oneself. A person who is not at home within himself is diseased. He is only healthy when he is at home there.

A young woman asked me, "What is the root cause of this ambition?"

I answered, "An inferiority complex, a feeling of poverty."

Certainly, an inferiority complex and ambition appear to be opposites, but are they really contradictory? No. They are not contradictory but rather two ends of the same feeling. What is an inferiority complex at one end is ambition at the other. Inferiority becomes ambition in its attempt to free itself from inferiority. It is inferiority all dressed up. But even after putting on the most valuable clothes it is neither eliminated nor destroyed. It may be that it is hidden from others, but the self keeps seeing it constantly. When a person is covered with clothes he is not naked to others' eyes, but he still is to himself.

That is the reason why those whose ambitious achievements dazzle the eyes of others will remain worried inside themselves and continue planning for greater successes. Their inner inferiority complex is not destroyed by success. Indeed, every new success comes to them as a new challenge for further successes. In this way, the successes that they had thought would be solutions prove only to be harbingers of newer problems. And this happens whenever one of life's problems is dealt with in a wrong way: the solutions to the problems become, in themselves, greater problems.

It is important to remember that covering up a disease is no escape from it. In this way diseases do not go away; they just get nourished. The mind, in its attempt to cover up a troublesome inferiority complex, gets filled with ambition and forgets it. It is also easy to forget oneself in the feeling of ambition. Then, whether the ambition is worldly or for enlightenment makes no difference. Ambition is intoxicating. Its intoxication brings deep self-forgetfulness. But once a person becomes used to intoxication or to a dose of intoxication, he no longer becomes intoxicated so easily, and the mind will need stronger and stronger doses of intoxicants and new ones too, and ambitions will keep on increasing. There will be no end to them. They have a beginning, but no end.

And when a person gets bored with worldly ambitions, or when his death is approaching, so-called religious ambitions will begin. These are also illusory, and the reality is that they will be more deeply intoxicating, because it is not so easy to see when you have achieved a religious goal and so the fear of failing will also be less.

As long as a person tries to keep himself separate from his authentic self, he will suffer from the fever of ambition in some form or another. In striving to be different from his true self, he will try to cover it and forget it. But is covering up a fact and becoming free from it the same thing? Is forgetting something and giving it up the same thing? No.

Forgetting an inferiority complex and becoming free from it are not the same. So this is a very unwise response because as you proceed with the treatment the disease will still be growing.

Every success of the ambitious mind is self-destructive, because it serves as fuel for the fire of ambition. Success is achieved, but the inferiority does not diminish so bigger successes become necessary and unavoidable. Basically, this is tantamount to increasing your inferiority complex.

The entire history of mankind is full of such diseased minds. What else do Tamberlaine, Alexander the Great and Hitler have? And please do not laugh at this comment, because it is not polite to laugh at the sick. It is also undesirable to laugh for another reason; and that is because the germs of their sickness are present in all of us. We are their inheritors – not only individuals, but the whole of humanity is sick with ambition. That is why this colossal disease escapes our attention.

In my opinion, an unavoidable characteristic of good mental health is a life free from ambition. Ambition is a disease and, therefore, it is destructive. Diseases are always the fellow-travelers of death. Ambition is destruction, it is violence, it is hatred coming out of a diseased mind, it is jealousy, it is a chronic struggle between man and man, it is war.

Even the ambition for enlightenment is destructive. It is violence against the self. It becomes enmity with the self itself. Worldly ambition is violence against others; ambition for enlightenment is violence against the self. Where there is ambition there is violence – it is another matter whether it is outward or inward. Violence, in every state or form, is always destructive. That is why only those understandings that arise from a healthy and calm mind can be creative.

A healthy mind is centered in the self: the urge to be something different will not be there. In the effort to be something different, the individual is not able to know himself – and not to know the self is the basic and central weakness from which all inferiority complexes are born.

There is no salvation from this weakness except getting to know the self. It is not through ambition, but only through knowing the self that we are freed from this desire, and for that to happen it is absolutely necessary to eliminate ambitions from the mind.

I am reminded of an anecdote about Tamberlaine and Baizad...

King Baizad was defeated in a battle and was brought before the conqueror, Tamberlaine. On seeing him, Tamberlaine suddenly started laughing out loud. Thereupon, the insulted Baizad proudly lifted his head and said, "Tamberlaine, do not be so arrogant about your victory in this battle. Remember, he who laughs at the defeat of others will one day have to shed tears at his own defeat."

King Baizad had only one eye and Tamberlaine had only one leg. On hearing the words of the one-eyed Baizad, the lame Tamberlaine laughed twice as much again and said, "I am not so foolish as to laugh at this small victory. I am laughing at our condition, yours and mine! See, you are one-eyed and I am lame. I was laughing at the thought of why God grants kingdoms to you and me who are one-eyed and lame."

I want to tell Tamberlaine, who is asleep in his grave, that this is not the fault of God. In fact, except for the lame and the one-eyed, no one else is eager for kingdoms. And isn't this true? Isn't it true that on the day man's mind becomes healthy there will be no kingdoms? Isn't it true that those who become healthy have always lost their kingdoms?

Whenever he finds any inferiority within himself man wants to run away. He starts running in exactly the opposite direction to it, and herein lies his mistake – because inferiority is no more than an indication of inner poverty.

Deep down, every person suffers from inner poverty. The same emptiness is felt by everyone. Attempts are made to fill up this inner emptiness with outer gains, but how can the pit of inner emptiness be filled from the outside? The outer is unable to do so for the very reason that it is on the outside, it cannot fill up the inner. After all, everything is on the outside – wealth, status, personality, power, religion, charity, renunciation, knowledge, God, salvation – so what is inside? Apart from poverty, emptiness, and nothingness, there is nothing inside. So if we run away from that nothingness we are running away from the real self: running away is running away from the essential being of the self.

The way is not to run away from it, but to live with it. For the person who has the courage to live and be alert, that emptiness is filled. For him, that emptiness itself proves to be his great salvation. In that nothingness everything exists. In that emptiness dwells existence, and that existence is godly.

Just Ten Steps Ahead 9

I am extremely surprised to see you all looking so worried about life. Life is not understood by just thinking about it; it can be understood only by living it to the full. There is no other way to know the truth.

Wake up and live! Wake up and move! Truth is not something dead that can be found without any effort. It is an extremely alive current. Only the person who moves with it, freely and without restraint, can find it. In thinking far ahead we often lose sight of that which is close at hand. What is under our noses all the time is the truth, and what is at a distance is hidden within it. Isn't it unavoidable that we have to discover that which is close by, in order to discover that which is at a distance? Doesn't the entire future exist in the present moment? Doesn't the smallest step contain within it the biggest journey ahead?

A simple farmer was going to the hills for the first time in his life. Although those hills were not very far away from his village, even so he had never been able to climb them. The summits of the hills, covered with green foliage, could be seen from his fields, and very often the desire to see them at close quarters would become very strong in him. But, for one reason or another, the journey had been postponed and he had not been able to get there.

The last time, he had been deterred for the simple reason that he had no lamp with him, and in order to reach the hills it was necessary to set out at night. The difficult climb up to the hills was even more problematic after sunrise. But on this occasion he had brought a lamp, and he was so excited about going to the hills that he did not sleep at all during the first part of the night.

He got up at two o'clock in the morning and started for the hills. But as soon as he had left the village he hesitated and then stopped. He started worrying and a concern developed in his mind. On coming out of the village he immediately noticed that it was a new moon night and all around it was pitch dark. Certainly he had a lamp with him, but the light of that lamp could not show him further than ten steps ahead and the climb was about ten miles long.

He was thinking that he had to go ten miles but the light that he was carrying could show him only ten steps ahead. How could that be enough? And was it advisable to go further into the pitch darkness with the light of just that small lamp? That would be like setting off across the sea in a very small boat. He sat outside the village to wait for the sunrise.

But as he was sitting there, an old man, who was going towards the hills, passed by. He was carrying an even smaller lamp in his hand. The farmer stopped the old man, and when he had told him of his doubts the old man started laughing loudly and said, "You madman! Just walk ten paces to begin with – walk as far as you can see. Then you will start seeing the same amount again. If you can see just one step you can go round the entire world with the help of that amount of light."

The young man understood, got up and started moving, and before the sun had come up he was already in the hills.

That old man's advice is worth remembering even on the path of life. I also want to say the same thing to you. Friends, why do you sit tight? Get up and move! It is not he who thinks, but he who moves who reaches. And let it be remembered that everyone has enough discernment and illumination to see ten steps ahead – and that is enough. That is enough to reach to godliness.

10   Unbreakable and Unending Love

Love is energy, and only the person who lives by love is, in fact, alive.

Where there is love there is godliness, because love is the light produced by the presence of the divine.

You may recall that whenever your mind is full of hatred, you become powerless and your connection with existence becomes weak. It is for this reason that unhappiness and regret are born out of anger, hatred, and jealousy. The state of remorse is born when one's own roots are separated from the existence of the whole.

Love fills you with happiness, with bliss, and with a music and compassion and a fragrance that do not belong to this material world. Why? Because, in this experience you become so close to the universal soul that you find a place in the heart of existence; as existence starts manifesting through you, you are no longer just yourself.

Therefore I say that the person who can find unbreakable and unending love in life finds everything.

I am reminded of an incident…

Mohammed was traveling along a road with his disciple, Ali.

An enemy of Ali came by, stopped him, and started insulting him.

Ali patiently listened to his abuses, his eyes showing love and prayer-fulness. He was listening to the poisoned talk of his enemy as if his enemy were praising him. His patience was tremendous, but finally he lost patience, and he came down to the level of the enemy and started retaliating. Gradually his eyes filled with anger and clouds of hatred and revenge started thundering in his heart. His hand was already reaching for his sword…

Until then, Mohammed was sitting calmly by, watching all of this. Suddenly he got up and moved away in another direction, leaving Ali and his enemy where they were. Seeing this, Ali was very surprised and also felt a little upset with Mohammed.

Later on, when Mohammed met up with him again, he asked, "Please explain this behavior of yours. The enemy confronted me, and you went away leaving me alone? Wasn't it like leaving me in the jaws of death?"

Mohammed replied, "Beloved one, that man was undoubtedly very violent and cruel, and his words were also full of towering rage. But I was very happy when I saw you at peace and being loving. At that stage, I saw that the ten bodyguards sent by God were defending you and his good wishes were raining down upon you. You were safe on account of your love and forgiveness. But as soon as your heart lost all compassion and became hard, and your eyes started producing flames of revenge, I saw those heavenly bodyguards leave you. At that moment it was only right that I should also leave you. God himself had left your company."

11   Search within Yourself

I ask everyone what they are looking for in life. The meaning and value of life is hidden in the inquiry into life itself. If a person is searching only for pearls and precious stones, how can the value of his life be greater than that for which he is searching? Most people become small by looking for the small, and in the end they find that they have wasted the treasure of their lives searching for some wealth that was, in fact, no wealth at all.

It is best, before we start on a journey, to find out where we want to reach, why we want to go, and also whether we will be able to put up with the difficulties and hard work that will be involved on the journey towards that goal. The person who does not think before setting out often finds that either he does not reach anywhere at all or that if he does reach somewhere, he does not find that place worth reaching.

I do not want such a mistake to happen in your lives because it will destroy your very life. Life is short. Energy is limited. Time is short. Therefore, only those who move after careful consideration and who are watchful and cautious can reach somewhere.

There was a mystic. His name was Shivli. He was on a journey. On his way, he saw a young man running fast and asked him, "My friend, where are you running to?"

Without stopping the young man said, "To my home."

Thereupon Shivli put rather a strange question to him. He asked, "Which home?"

I am also asking you the same question. You are running away. All of you are running away. I am asking: Where are you running to? Could it be that this entire race is not planned? Aren't you running because everyone else is running – without knowing where you have to reach?

I wish that in reply to this question you could say the same thing as that young man said to Shivli. Then my whole being would start dancing with happiness. The young man said, "There is only one home: the house of God. I am in search of that."

Without a doubt, everything else is a dream. The search for any other home is a dream. There is only one home; the real home is only one – the house of God – and he who searches for it has to go within himself because it is hidden in the self. Is there any house other than the house of the divine, and can the divine be found anywhere except within the self?

If I had been in Shivli's place, I would have asked that young man who was running one more question. I do not know what answer he would have given. But let me tell you the question itself.

I would have asked him: Friend, if you want to find the divine why are you running away? Where are you running to? How will you find that which exists right here by running away? Isn't it an illusion to want to reach the divine in the future when it exists in the here and now? And the fact is that which already exists inside can only be lost by running away. To find it, isn't it best to stop, stay still, and search within yourself?

12   Swim in the Sea of Truth

Do not search for religion; search for yourself. Then religion will automatically come to you.

Does religion exist in the scriptures? No. Religion does not exist in the scriptures. Scriptures are dead, and religion is a living entity. How can it be found in the scriptures?

Does religion exist within religious organizations? No. Religion does not exist even within religious sects. Organized religion is dependent on agreements, and religion is an absolutely individual affair. To attain it, it is not necessary to go outside. You have to move inside.

Religion exists in our every breath. All that we lack is the vision to uncover and see it.

Religion exists in our every drop of blood. We lack the courage and determination to seek it out.

Religion is here, like the sun, but you have to open your eyes.

Religion is life, but you have to rise above the graveyard of the body.

Religion is not lifeless. Therefore, do not sleep. Wake up and move! The one who sleeps, loses it. The one who moves on, attains it. The one who is awake, finds it.

A king was searching for the greatest religion in the world. He had grown from youth into old age but still he had not finished his research. How could it be completed? Life is brief and such research is foolish. Even if life were endless the best religion could still not be discovered because, in fact, religion is simply religion and it is all one. For this very reason, what could be higher or lower, what could be the best or the worst? Because there are not many religions, the search for the greatest one cannot be successful. Where there are not many, where there is only one, there is no scope for comparison or for weighing up, nor is there any method for doing so. That king was searching for the highest religion but living in the lowest irreligious state.

As long as he was unable to find true religion, the question of living a religious life in accordance with it did not arise for him. Does anyone ever move into darkness and into the unknown? No one ever asks such a question about irreligion, but there will be hardly anyone who has not asked it about religion. Nobody ever thinks about or researches irreligion. Rather, irreligion is lived while religion is researched. Most probably this so-called search is a way to live in the opposite direction from religion, and in that way avoid living religiously.

Nobody ever told the king about this. The scholars, the saints and the philosophers of different religions used to come to him. They quarreled with one another. They would highlight one another's faults. They would prove that the others were ignorant. The king used to enjoy all this. In this way, religion became an illusion and full of ignorance in his eyes, and he could find an excuse for living in the opposite way from it.

It was difficult to win the king over onto the side of religion – because whoever takes sides is himself not in favor of religion. Groups, sects and religious institutions are always promoting their own sides. They have nothing to do with religion; they cannot have. Only one who is on no one's side can be religious. Without giving up sides it is difficult to be religious. Religious sects are ultimately enemies of religiousness and friends of its very opposite.

So the king did not give up his research: it had become his play. But eventually even the opposite of religion began to bring him pain, anxiety, and misery. As death came closer and the twilight years of his life approached, he became restless. But still, he was not prepared to accept anything but the highest, internally faultless, and complete religion. He was adamant and determined that until he had become clear what the perfect religion was, he would not to take even one step of his life towards it. Year after year went by, and he was getting himself more and more deeply into the mud. Death had almost reached his door.

Then one day a young beggar came to his gate and asked for alms, and finding the king extremely worried, depressed and perturbed, asked him the reason. The king replied, "How could you help me even if I explained? The greatest scholars, saints and wandering monks have not been able to help me."

The beggar then said, "It is possible that their greatness was in itself a barrier for them? And in any case scholars have never been able to do anything. Are saints and monks who can only be identified by their clothes really the ones who matter?"

The king looked at the beggar attentively. The king had a look in his eyes, which was not in the eyes of the beggar. That look can be seen only in the eyes of a king.

Meanwhile, the beggar spoke again, "I can do nothing. In fact, I do not exist. But the one who exists can do a lot."

What he was saying was truly wonderful. He was entirely different from the thousands who had come to try and convince the king. The king started thinking to himself, "Who is this man who is dressed in such poor clothes?" but out loud he said, "I wanted to seek out the highest religion and make my life religious, but this has not been possible and

I am therefore very unhappy as I am now coming to the end of my life. Which religion is the highest?"

The beggar started laughing loudly and said, "Oh king! You have wanted to put the cart before the horse. That is why you are unhappy. Life does not become religious *after* you have found religion; religion is found only when life itself becomes religious. And what madness was it that prompted you to seek out the highest religion? Just seeking religion itself is enough. Only *religion* exists. The *highest* religion? I have never heard of it. Such words are meaningless. Nothing needs to be added to qualify religion. There is only a circle. There is no such thing as a full circle, because whatever is not a full circle is not a circle at all. Just being a circle implies its fullness. The very existence of religion implies the truth of its being impartial and faultless. And those who come to you to demonstrate the highest religion are either no less mad than you or they are hypocrites. One who knows, knows only religion, religiousness – and not religions.

The king was deeply moved and touched the beggar's feet. The beggar said, "Kindly leave my feet alone. Do not bind them. I have come here to free your feet. Please come to the other side of the river outside your kingdom. There, I can point my finger towards religion."

They went together to the riverbank. The best available boats were brought to them but the beggar would point out one fault after another in each one of them. Eventually the king became frustrated. He said to the beggar, "Oh, great soul! We have only to cross this small river. We can even swim across. Let us forget about these boats. Let us get there by swimming across. Why waste our time?"

As if the beggar had been waiting for this, he said to the king, "Oh king! I also wanted to say the same thing. Why are you so concerned with the boats that belong to different religious sects? Isn't it best for us to swim across to God? In fact, there is no religious boat. Boats are only for boatmen. The only way is for us to swim. Truth can be found only through our own efforts. Nobody else can give it to us. One has to swim in the sea of truth by oneself. There is no other support. Those who look for support will drown close to the shore, but those who take courage and swim by themselves will manage to cross, even if they have a little taste of drowning at the beginning."

Each Life Is an Original Creation 13

A child asked me, "I want to become like the Buddha; can you show me how to reach to my ideal?" That child was very old. He had seen at least sixty springs. But anyone who wants to become like others is still a child and has not yet become mature.

Is it not the sign of maturity that, rather than wanting to be like others, a person wishes to become himself? And if someone wants to become like someone else, will he ever be able to do so?

A person can only be himself. It is impossible to become like someone else.

When I call that old man a boy, you laugh. But if you probe a little more deeply, you will not laugh, you will weep, because you will find that same childish mentality exists even in you. Don't you want to be like somebody else? Do you have the courage and maturity within to be your own self?

If everyone were mature, then the question of trying to follow someone else would not arise. Isn't it because of this childlike mentality that the following and the followed, the disciple and the teacher, have come into existence? And remember: the mind that wants to follow is not only immature, it is also blind.

What did I tell that old boy?

I said to him: Friend, the person who wants to become like someone else loses himself. Every seed contains within itself its own tree, and it is the same with each individual. It is only possible to become oneself. If a person tries to become anything else it is possible he may not even become what his own potential was.

Seek out who you are. That is where the growth towards that which you *can* become lies hidden. Other than that, there is no ideal for anybody. In the name of ideals people get deflected from the path of self-development and reach nowhere. I see suicides behind the copying of these ideals – and there can be nothing but suicides. What am I doing whenever I try to be like someone else? I am killing my own self, I am suppressing myself – and I will come to hate myself. So, the result will be suicide and hypocrisy because I will be pretending to be what I am not: to look, appear, and behave as I am not.

As soon as duality develops inside an individual, hypocrisy sets in. Wherever there is self-contradiction within, there is falsehood, there is irreligion – and it is only natural that such an unnatural endeavor should bring pain, anxiety, and remorse. Done excessively, such tensions become a hell for people. Unless an ideal is born out of a self-realized truth, out of self-realized possibilities and the discipline that automatically follows like their shadow, everything else makes a person ugly and deformed. Any frameworks or ideals or discipline that are imported from the outside, are suicidal.

So I say: search for yourself and find yourself. This is the door to existence, where only those who find themselves are welcome. Through that door the godly may pass but the Ram – the god, the hero – in a Ram–Leela play cannot. Whenever someone, inspired by external ideals, wants to mold himself, he is behaving like the Ram in a Ram–Leela drama. That some may succeed more, and some less is a separate issue, but ultimately the more successful a person is, the further away he is from his self. The success of the Rams in Ram–Leela plays is, in fact, the failure of their own beings.

You can use Ram, Buddha or Mahavira as a covering, and, whoever puts such coverings on has no music, independence, beauty or truth in his individuality. Existence will treat him in the same way that the king of Sparta treated a man who had become so good at imitating the voice of the *bulbul* bird that he had forgotten the voice of man...

This man had become very famous and people from far and wide came to listen to him. He wanted to demonstrate his skill even before the king. After making great efforts he gained permission to appear before him. He thought that the king would praise him and honor him with a reward. This expectation of his was not unjustified given the praise and rewards he had been getting from others.

But what did the king say to him? He said, "Sir, I have heard the *bulbul* singing, but I expect you to sing not the songs of the *bulbul* but the songs for which you have been born. There are enough *bulbuls* to sing the *bulbuls'* songs. Go and prepare your own song, and when you have prepared it come to see me again. I will be ready to welcome you and there will also be a reward waiting for you."

Surely, life is not given to us to imitate others but to develop the tree that is hidden within the seed of our own beings. Life is not an imitation, it is an original creation.

14   Spiritual Pride

A temple is under construction. I pass by and think to myself that as there are already many temples and the number of people visiting them has probably gone down why is this new temple being built? And this is not the only one: there are many other new temples under construction. A few new temples are being built every day.

Temples are being built and the number of people visiting them is going down. What is the reason for this? I thought about this a lot, but could not arrive at an answer. Then I asked an elderly mason who was building a temple. I thought he might know the mystery behind the construction of so many new temples because he had built so many of them himself.

The old man started laughing at my question and then he took me behind the temple where the stones were being chiseled. Right there, statues of God were also being made. I thought that perhaps he would say that the temple was being constructed for those statues of God. But this would not satisfy my curiosity, because then the question would arise why these statues were being made.

But no, I was mistaken. He did not say anything about those statues.

He walked past them, and kept moving on. At the far end, beyond everything else, some artisans were working on a stone. The old man showed me the stone and said, "It is for this that the temple is being constructed – and temples have always been constructed for this." I was stunned and started regretting my foolishness. Why hadn't I thought of this earlier? On that stone, they were engraving the name of the person who was getting the temple built.

Thinking about this on my way home, I saw a procession moving along the road. Someone had renounced the world and become a sann-yasin. The procession was in his honor. I stood by the roadside and started watching. I looked at the face and into the eyes of the person who had renounced. The emptiness often found in the eyes of a sannyasin was not present in his eyes. In his there existed the same ego and greatness that can be seen in the eyes of politicians.

Could it be possible that I was mistaken, and my thought was only there because of the effect the conversation with that old mason had had on me? But I know many other sannyasins, and the subtle form of ego that you can see in them is difficult to find elsewhere. Perhaps any action that originates from man's mind is not without ego. Unless you can get free from the mind, there is no escape from a sense of greatness.

Only a few days ago, a friend kept up a fast for ten days. I was very surprised to see how anxious he was to advertise his fast. But no, that was my mistake: that old mason uncovered misunderstandings that I had had my whole life...

After the fast, that friend was given a big reception and praise was heaped on him. I was also there, and a man whispered in my ears, "Poor fellow, he has borne the entire expenditure of this reception."

At the time I was startled, but because of that old mason, I am wiser today and see no reason for surprise. On the contrary, one thought haunts me again and again: if self-advertisement is so useful in this world why shouldn't it also be in heaven? Won't the rules of heaven be the same as the ones here? After all, heaven is a creation of the same mind that creates this world. Isn't the desire for, and conception of, heaven the same as other desires of the mind? Then who is this God? Isn't he an invention of man's mind? After all he also feels insulted and angry, and out of revenge roasts his enemies in the fires of hell. He also feels happy when given praise; he saves his devotees from troubles and showers them with blessings. Isn't all this also a creation of man's mind? And if all this is so then why shouldn't advertising succeed in God's world too? Shouldn't God also be counting fame as proof of his existence? After all, what other yardstick could man use for him?

I shared this same view with a sannyasin, and he became very angry, "What are you thinking? What need is there for religion to advertise? Everything is an ego game: everything in this world is *maya*, a divine play. Because of their ignorance people's lives remain caught up in the ego."

I accepted everything he was saying: that renunciation leads to knowledge, and because he had renounced everything he possessed, he must have found knowledge. How could I possibly doubt his words? But in a short space of time he reminded me two or three times that he had turned his back on his wealth which had amounted to hundreds of thousands of rupees in order to become a sannyasin. In other words, he was no ordinary sannyasin!

Even renunciation is measured with money.

I asked him, "When did you turn your back on all this?"

He said, "About twenty-five or thirty years ago." In that moment it was worth seeing the way his eyes were shining. The saying that renunciation brings a certain shine to the eyes seemed true.

Very hesitantly I said to him, "Sir, perhaps you did not kick it away strongly enough, otherwise, how could the memory of that day still be so fresh, even after thirty years?"

And what I had feared finally happened. His anger burst out. But I consoled myself with the thought that this is an old habit of the seers and the sages, and he was compassionate enough not to also put some sort of curse on me!

At the time of my departure, I told him a story. I will repeat it to you. Think it over carefully. It is full of meaning.

A rich man offered ten thousand gold coins to Shree Nathji, the presiding deity of the Nathdwara temple. But he started counting the gold coins one by one before placing them in front of the idol. He poured them energetically out of the bag and with a lot of jangling. On hearing that jangling sound a crowd gathered in the temple. He started making still more noise by counting the coins. As the crowd increased, his enjoyment in his renunciation increased.

At last, when he had finished counting the coins and, with pride in his eyes, was looking at the people assembled there, the priest spoke to him, "Brother, take these coins away. Shree Nathji will not accept such an offering."

The rich man was amazed. He asked, "Why not, sir?"

The priest replied, "Can love be demonstrated? Is prayerfulness a thing to show to others? In fact, in your heart there is the desire to advertise. Such a desire is incapable of gratitude, such a desire is unable to let go. Such a desire is unqualified to love."

15   "I" Is an Untruth

A devotee, who was in great mental torment, asked me, "I want to lose myself in the *brahman*. Ego is painful; I want to offer this ego to God. What should I do?"

I know this man. For years he has been going to the temple. With his head at God's feet he has wept for hours. His desire is certainly very intense, but his direction is wrong, because a person who accepts the "I" becomes the "I" on account of that very acceptance. From this "I" follows pain – and then he wants to get rid of the pain and wants to offer himself into the care of God.

But the central core of this offer is also the "I" – because who is it that wants to offer? Who is it that wants to get rid of all the pain and trouble? Is it not the "I" itself? Whose is this anxiety and urge for God, for utter happiness and for the ultimate? Who is it that makes you race in this world and then also excites you with the idea of salvation? Is it not the "I" itself?

I ask: is it possible for the "I" to give itself up? I want to offer myself. Won't the "I" be involved in this? Is not my offer also "mine"? Doesn't whatever is "mine" give birth to "mine" or "I"? Doesn't my wealth, my possessions, my wife, don't my children all produce this "I"? My sannyas, my renunciation, my offering, my charity, my religion, my soul, my salvation also produce this "I."

As long as any part of the "mine" remains, the "I" will remain completely intact. Every action of the "I" – be it sin or piety, indulgence or renunciation – only serves to strengthen the "I." Even if you make great efforts or try to give it up, the only result will be to strengthen it.

Is there no way, then, to drop the ego? Is there no method to renounce it? No, there is no way or method of giving up, renouncing, or offering up the ego, because whatever is done will ultimately prove to be life-enhancing for the ego. No one has ever gone beyond the ego through action, deeds, or resolve, nor can they ever go beyond it in this way because the resolve itself is the ego in a small form. Resolve is the unripe form of ego. After ripening, it is transformed into the ego. The ego is the consolidated form of a resolve.

So how can the ego be dropped with the help of resolve? And what are all our attempts and offerings? Aren't they all just extensions of resolve?

Attempts to free yourself from the ego *with* the ego are as foolish as trying to pull yourself up by your own bootstraps. In fact, the ego cannot be given up, because, if it is there, nothing else can exist alongside it. And if it doesn't exist, then it doesn't, and any question of dropping it will not arise. That is why I say that it is important that the ego is known, not by surrender but through knowledge, not by meditation but though knowledge, not by renunciation but through knowledge. And the wonder of wonders is that while it gets nourished through effort or surrender, through knowledge it cannot be found at all!

To know the "I," the ego, in its entirety is to become free from it.

The "I," the ego, cannot be given up because in reality it does not exist. Lies, falsehoods, have to be invented in order to try – unsuccessfully – to lose what is not there.

The ego is an untruth. When trying to give it up, another untruth – that of "surrender" – has to be invented, and then to support the untruth of surrender, another untruth – "God" – has to be created by the imagination. But from such untruths there is no salvation. On the contrary, bigger untruths are let loose.

A holy man found an orphan boy by the roadside. He brought him up until he was an adult.

There was a graveyard just behind his hut, and as the child was very mischievous, he would often go to the graveyard during the day or at night. To make sure that he didn't go there, the holy man told him. "Don't go there at night. Ghosts live there and they eat people up."

Naturally, from that day, the child started being afraid of the graveyard and avoiding it. Then he was sent to the *gurukul*, the forest university, and there, too, he also felt afraid of being alone and of the dark.

After several years he returned home. By then he had grown into a young man, but his fear had grown with him. One night, the holy man asked him to cross the graveyard and go to the village on an errand. But the young man started trembling at the very thought of crossing the graveyard at night, and replied, "How can I go there in darkness? That place is haunted by ghosts who eat people up."

The holy man laughed; he tied an amulet around the young man's arm and said, "Now you can go. Now, the ghosts will not be able to harm you. Because of this amulet God will always protect you and be with you, and because of God, the ghosts will no longer be able to appear before you. With God by your side, how can you fear the ghosts?"

So the young man went, and not finding any ghosts there, it was easily proved to him that God was omnipotent. In this way, the ghosts had disappeared, but God had entered in, and God, who had been brought in to drive away the ghosts, could, of course, only become a bigger ghost.

The young man, with the help of God, was now freed from the ghosts, but now he could not be separated from the amulet even for a moment.

It was inevitable that he would feel afraid of the God who could terrify even ghosts. He became afraid that God would desert him because of some of his faults, failures, or crimes. And if that happened, the ghosts would surely take their full revenge on him. For that reason, he started to worship and pray to God. Not only did he start worshipping God but at the same time he also began to fear God's representatives and brokers on this earth.

On seeing all this, the holy man was upset. His remedy had created an even more serious problem. Those poor ghosts were far better than this God. The ghosts would only tease people in the graveyard in the darkness of the night, but this God was after the young man even in the light of day! On the new moon night, the holy man pulled the amulet off the young man's arm and threw it into the oven.

The young man started trembling and his face grew pale. He would have fainted, but the holy man supported him and then told him the whole story of how the ghosts, and then later God, had been invented to give him support. When the young man felt slightly convinced, the holy man took him to the graveyard. They searched every nook and corner of that graveyard. The young man was surprised because there was not a ghost to be found anywhere.

In this way the ghosts – and also God – disappeared. The young man felt relieved and free from fear.

In fact a thorough search for ghosts and their abodes only leads to freedom from them.

The ego produces pain, brings torture, gives birth to anxiety and feelings of being unsafe, and creates the fear of death. So to find an escape from all of this, the idea of surrendering to God was invented. It is out of this fear that God and worship are born, and meanwhile the ego does not really exist at all. As long as we do not search for it and know this, it will exist. It has no existence except in our ignorance – and how can that which does not exist be surrendered? If ghosts do not exist, what is there to escape from? Because the ghosts exist God is needed. Because the ego exists, surrender to God is necessary. Discover the ghosts of the ego, and not the amulet given to protect you against them.

Dive inside yourself and find where this ego exists. As soon as you start searching for it you will find that it does not exist. The graveyard is empty of ghosts, the being inside the self is empty of ego. Then what remains is godliness, what is experienced is true surrender, and what exists is *brahman*.

The Poison of Faith 16

An old woman was very sick. As she lived alone in her house she was in great difficulty. One day, early in the morning, two nice women, who appeared to be very religious, came to see her. They had henna markings on their hands and strings of prayer beads. They started helping the old woman and said, "With God's grace everything will be all right. Faith is power, and it never goes to waste."

That simple old woman trusted them – more so because she was alone, and a person who lives alone wants to trust people. She was in pain, and when people are in trouble they trust easily. These unknown women looked after her the whole day. Because of their help and their religious discussions throughout the day, the old lady's confidence in them grew still stronger.

At nighttime, following the instructions of those women, she lay down beneath a blanket so they could offer a prayer to God for her health. Incense was burned; sweet-smelling water was sprinkled around, and one of the women, with her hands on the old woman's head, started reciting some unknown mantras. Later, to the sweet music of the mantras, the old woman was lulled to sleep.

At midnight she woke up. The house was in darkness. When she lit the lamp, she found that those unknown ladies had left her a long time ago. The doors of the house were wide open, and her safe had been broken into. Her trust had indeed borne fruit – not only for herself, but for those two crooks! And there is nothing surprising in this, because faith has always been fruitful for crooks.

Religion is not faith; it is discernment. It is not blindness; it is a treatment for the ego. But discernment is an obstacle for those who want to exploit, and, that is why they administer the poison of faith.

Thinking is a revolt, and because exploitation of a revolutionary is impossible, people are educated in a "faith." Thinking makes a person free, makes him an individual. But for exploitation you need sheep, you need weak-minded followers. So thinking is murdered and faith is nurtured.

Man is helpless, and therefore, in his helplessness, in his loneliness, he accepts faith. Life is painful, and, therefore, to run away from it, one rests in the lap of any faith or belief. This state of affairs definitely offers a golden opportunity to the exploiters and the selfish. Religion is in the hands of the crooks, and, that is why there is irreligion in the world. So long as religion is not free from faith, real religion cannot be born.

Only when religion is combined with the ferocity of discernment will there be freedom, will truth and power will be born. Religion is power because thinking is power. Religion is light. Religion is light because intellect is light. Religion is freedom because discernment is freedom.

Freedom, Freedom, Freedom!   17

Religion, religion, religion! Religion is talked about so much, but what is the result? I hear everyone quoting from the scriptures, but what is the result? Man is still drowning in pain and misery and we are just repeating the principles we have been taught. Life is deteriorating every moment towards animalism, and here we are, bowing our heads – as always – in temples made of stones.

Perhaps we are so involved in words, in lifeless words, that we have lost the power to see the truth. Our minds are so bound to the scriptures that we have lost the power to discover for ourselves. And perhaps that is the reason why there is an unbridgeable gulf between thought and action. And maybe, for the same reason, we keep living in exactly the opposite way to what we say to want. The wonder is that this contradiction is not even noticed by us!

Have we not become blind, even though our eyes are still intact?

I ponder over this condition and find that it is those very truths – that have not been discovered by people for themselves – that are dragging us into such confusion. Truth, if discovered by the self, leads to freedom. If it does not come from the self, it ties us up in still tighter bonds.

There is no greater untruth than the truths that are taught by others. Such borrowed truths will produce very troublesome contradictions in life.

There was a domesticated parrot living in a hillside inn. The parrot would repeat, day and night, what his master had taught him. He used to say, "Freedom, freedom, freedom!"

A traveler came to stay at the inn for the first time. The parrot's words touched him deeply. He had been arrested several times while fighting for the freedom of his country, and when the parrot, breaking the utter silence of the hills, would shout, "Freedom, freedom, freedom!" an echo resounded within the man's heart. He would remember the days of his imprisonment and would remember that his own inner being used to cry in that very same way, "Freedom, freedom, freedom!"

When night fell, the traveler got up and tried to free the parrot who was calling out for his freedom. The traveler tried pulling the parrot out of his cage but the parrot was not ready to come out. Quite the reverse, he held tightly on to the bars of the cage and shouted even more loudly, "Freedom, freedom, freedom!"

With great difficulty, the traveler was finally able to get the parrot out. After setting him free in the outside air, the traveler fell fast asleep.

But when he got up in the morning, he saw that the parrot was sitting happily inside his cage crying, "Freedom, freedom, freedom!"

Fearlessness   18

I have heard a story. It was during the war, and a bombardment suddenly started. A priest, who was walking somewhere along a lonely path, started running for safety, and took shelter in a cave in which wolves lived. As soon as he entered the cave he saw that a military officer was already hiding there. The officer moved to one side so that there could be more room for the newcomer. Then bombs were falling all around and the priest started trembling. He sat in the lotus posture and started praying to God. He was praying loudly.

When he looked up, he found that the military officer was praying as loudly as he was. When the attack ended, the priest said, "Brother, I saw that you were also praying."

The military officer started laughing and said, "Sir, how could an atheist sit in a cave of wolves?"

The first condition to find the truth is fearlessness.

And think about it: can fear ever become love? If fear cannot become love, how can it become prayer?

Prayer is the perfection of love.

But in the very foundations of the temples that are made by man lie bricks of fear, and the God carved out of fear is made with feelings of fear. It is for this reason that all that we possess is untrue – because what could be true for those whose God is not true?

And is it any wonder that the very breath of those whose thoughts are untrue, whose love is untrue, whose prayer is untrue is false?

Through love alone: prayer is true only when it comes out of love.

Are you also not searching for God out of fear? Are your prayers not also based on fear? Remember that a religion that is based on fear is not true religion. I prefer a fearless atheist to a theist who is afraid, because it is impossible to reach God through fear.

And through knowledge, and only through knowledge, can the God who *does* exist be known. I say love, and the intensity of love alone will convert your life into prayer. I say awaken your own intellect, because only its awakening will enable you to see the divine. Love and intellect: the person who has understood these two basic mantras can know all that should be known, is worth knowing, and can be known.

Where is the temple of God? When someone asks me this, I tell him that it is in love, in the intellect.

Surely, love is God, the intellect is God.

The Gates of Heaven 19

One day there was a big crowd at the gates of heaven.

Some priests were crying out, "Open the gates quickly!" But the gatekeepers told them; "Wait a little. Let us find out more about you, about whether the knowledge that you have accumulated comes from the scriptures or from your beings, because there is no value placed here on knowledge gathered from the scriptures."

In the meantime, a saint moved to the front of the crowd and said, "Open the gate! I want to enter heaven. I have done many fasts and penances. During my time, who was a greater performer of penances than I?"

The gatekeeper replied, "Swamiji, please wait a little. Let us find out why you performed these penances – because where there is the slightest wish for gain there is neither renunciation nor penance."

Just at that moment a few social workers arrived. They also wanted to enter heaven. But the gatekeeper told them, "You have also fallen into a big misunderstanding. The service that claims a reward is no service at all. Even so, we will find out more about you."

And then the eyes of one of the gatekeepers fell on a person who was standing in the shadows at the back. The crowd was asked to make way for that person. Tears were falling from the man's eyes. He said, "Undoubtedly, I have been brought here by mistake. Me, in heaven? I am an absolute fool. I do not know the scriptures at all. I am absolutely unaware of any renunciation, because how could I renounce anything when I had nothing of my own? I have never done any good works. When did I have the chance of doing them? Only love flows from my heart, but love is no qualification for entering heaven. And the truth is I don't want to enter heaven. Please be good enough to tell me the way to hell. Perhaps that is my place and I am needed there."

Soon after his speech the gatekeepers opened the gates of heaven and said, "You are blessed among mortals. You have gained immortality. The gates of heaven are already open for you. You are welcome."

Is it not one of God's prayers to be the last in the queue of life? Is it not a blessing to be last in life?

.

Attentiveness 20

It happened on a full-moon night. It was midnight, and surrounded by friends, I was in a boat on a lake. All around me were rocks bathed in moonlight. Everything was unbelievably beautiful. It seemed as if I was in a city of dreams. The boatman stopped rowing the boat and we became still in the middle of the lake.

But my friends were not there. They had brought me with them, but I could not tell whether they had been left behind or gone ahead. Even though I was surrounded by them, I was alone on that lake because they were all lost in many things, which I knew nothing about. Their talking related either to the past, which was not there, or to the future, which was also not there. But their consciousness was not there with them. They were not present for that wonderful lake and for that dreamlike night, just as if the present did not exist for them.

Then suddenly one of them asked, "Does God exist?" What answer could I give him? I pondered it, because how could they, who had no relationship with the aliveness of the present moment, have any relationship with God? Life itself is godliness. The realization of life is the realization of godliness. So I said to them, "Friends, is this a lake? Is this the moon? Is this the night? And aren't we all present on this lake in this wonderful full-moon night?"

Naturally, all of them were startled and said, "Yes. How can there be any question about that?"

But I continued, "For myself I have no doubt, but I am convinced that you are not here. Please think again. The person who is only present in the physical sense can only gather an idea of the physical existence of this world, but the one who is present with all his consciousness can experience godliness here and now. Godliness is present, but only for those who are attentive to it, for those who are really living."

Again, I was reminded of an incident and I told them about it…

A few people had collected outside an office. One of them was to be chosen for the post of wireless operator. All the applicants and candidates were busy discussing useless things. Then slowly some sounds started emanating from a transmitter, but they were all so engrossed and lost in their conversations that the low-level signals did not attract their attention.

But one young man was sitting apart from them, alone in a corner. He got up at once and went into the office. The rest of them did not see him getting up or going into the office. They observed him only when, with a smile, he came out of the office with an appointment letter in his hand.

Naturally, all of them were speechless and, in anger, they asked the young man, "Sir, how did you manage to get inside before everyone else? All of us were here much earlier than you. You were the last in the queue. How could you be appointed without us being considered first? What is this highhandedness? What is this injustice?"

At this, the young man started laughing and said, "Friends, how can I be blamed for this? Any one of you could have been appointed, and perhaps I have been appointed after each of you had been considered. Didn't you hear the message given out on the wireless?"

They all spoke with one voice, "What kind of message? What message?"

Then the young man told them, "Weren't you aware of the wireless signals? The sound produced on the transmitter clearly said, "I want a person who is always careful and attentive. The appointment letter is being kept ready for the person who hears this message and enters the office before anyone else."

God's messages are also raining down on us every day. Nature is the language of his signals. The person who is silent and attentive, who stays alert to these signals will definitely be invited in.

21   The Path of Love

Is love not God, and the heart, drowned in love, the temple? And isn't the person who gives up love and searches for God elsewhere searching in vain?

Once, I used to ask myself this; now I am asking you. The person searching for God is announcing that he has not attained love, because the person who attains love attains godliness as well.

The search for God is rooted in the need for love, but the fact is that it is impossible to find God without experiencing love first. And as this is so, the person who starts by seeking God will not find him, and will also be deprived of finding love. But the person who searches for love will ultimately find love and also, in the end, God.

Love is the path, love is the door, love is the energy that moves the feet; love is life's thirst, and, in the end, love is life's achievement. In truth, love is God.

I say: forget God and find love. Forget the temples and search in your heart – because if God exists, he is there. If there is any image of God, it is love. But that image has been lost among idols of stone. If there is any temple of God it is the heart, but the temple of the heart has been completely covered by temples of clay. God has been lost in the idols and temples made for him. It is difficult to meet him because of his priests. It has become impossible to hear his voice because of the sound of chants and prayers being sung to him.

If love returns to the life of man, God will also return with it.

A learned man went to visit a saint. He was carrying such a big bundle of scriptures on his head that by the time he reached the saint's hut he was almost dead. As soon as he arrived he asked the saint, "What do I need to do to meet God?"

The bundle that he had been carrying on his head was still there.

The saint said, "Friend, first of all you put down that bundle."

The learned man felt very reluctant. Even so, he took courage and put the load down. Without a doubt, you need unshakeable courage to throw off the loads that you carry in your soul. But even then he was keeping one hand on his bundle.

The saint said, "Friend, pull away that hand too."

That man must have been very courageous, because summoning all his energy he withdrew his hand from the bundle. Then the saint said, "Are you acquainted with love? Have your feet ever traveled on the path of love? If not, go and enter the temple of love. Live love and know it, and then come back. I can assure you that I will take you to God after that."

The learned man went back home. He had gone as a learned man but he no longer was. He had left his collection of knowledge behind. That man was surely unusual and blessed, because it is easier to give up thrones than to give up knowledge – after all, knowledge is the last support of the ego. But it is necessary to lose it for love.

The opposite of love is hatred. The main enemy of love is ego, and hatred is one of its children. Attachment, nonattachment, desire, freedom from desire, greed, hatred, jealousy, anger, enmity – are all its children. Ego's family is very large.

The saint went with that man to the outskirts of the village and bade him goodbye. The man deserved it: the saint was pleased with his courage. Where there is courage it is possible for religion to be born. Courage leads to freedom and freedom brings you face-to-face with truth.

But then the years rolled by. The saint became weary of waiting for the man's return, and he did not come back. Finally, the saint set off in search of him, and one day he found him. He was found, lost within himself, dancing in a village. It was difficult even to recognize him. Happiness had rejuvenated him. The saint stopped by him and asked, "Why didn't you come back? I got tired of waiting for you, so then I came here myself in search of you. Don't you want to search for God?"

The man said, "No; not at all. The moment I discovered love, in that very moment I found God too."

Many Types of Self-deception 22

A woman said, "I want to change myself. What shall I do?"

I said that the first thing to avoid was changing what you wear – because whenever a moment of self-transformation comes to people's lives their minds get caught up with changing their clothes. This is convenient for the mind; this is where its safety lies. By changing clothes, the mind does not die; on the contrary, wearing new clothes instead of old and worn-out ones prolongs its life.

By changing clothes there is no self-transformation; on the contrary, there is ego-fulfillment, and ego-fulfillment is suicide.

The woman asked me which clothes I meant.

I said, "There are many types of clothes, cover-ups, and many types of self-deception. You should beware of whatever can be put on as a cover. Whatever covers the reality of the self serves to deceive the self. I give the name *clothes* to such things. If a man is a sinner, he puts on the clothes of virtue; if a man is violent, he puts on the clothes of nonviolence; if a man is ignorant, he stuffs himself with words and scriptures and covers himself with this knowledge. It is an ancient trick of the irreligious mind to put on the clothes of religion in order to avoid religion."

I asked the woman if she couldn't see that what I was saying was always happening.

Then she thought for a bit and said, "I want to become a nun."

I said, "Now, know that the change of clothes has begun." Whenever a person wants to become something, the conspiracy of the mind has begun. The ambition to become something is the mind. This ambition wants to escape from what is real and to take cover behind what is not there. Ideals are the birth-givers of all covers and masks. A person who wants to know truth – and no self-transformation from the roots is possible without knowing truth – they will first have to know who they really are The revolution takes place not in desiring for something which is not, rather in the total unfolding of that which is. When a person comes to know the truth about his self in its totality, this knowing becomes the revolution, the transformation. In the revolution of knowing there is no gap of time. There is no time-gap in the revolution that arises from knowing. Where there is a gap in time there is no revolution, rather only a search for the changing of the cover."

Then I told her about an incident…

One day someone approached Abu Hasan and said, "Oh saint, the beloved of God, I am terrified of my sinful life and am determined to change myself. I want to become a saint. Will you not have compassion on me? Can you give me the holy clothes that you have been wearing? I also want to become holy by wearing them."

The man laid his head on Hasan's feet and drenched them with his tears. There was no room for doubting his intense desire – weren't his tears the witness?

Abu Hasan picked him up and said, "Friend, before I make the mistake of giving my clothes to you, can you also be kind enough to reply to a question of mine? Can a woman become a man by wearing a man's clothes, or is there any man who can become a woman by wearing a woman's clothes?"

That man wiped away his tears – perhaps he has come to a wrong place – and he said, "No."

Abu Hasan started laughing and said, "Here are my clothes. But what difference will it make even if you put on my skin? Has anyone ever become a saint by putting on a saint's clothes?"

And if I had been in Hasan's place, I would have said, "Has anyone ever become a saint even being inspired by the desire to become one? Saintliness comes. It is the fruit of knowing. And wherever there is a desire to be something there is no knowing, because a mind moved by desire becomes restless, and where can knowing be found in restlessness? Wherever there is a desire to become anything, there is an escape from the self. And how can a person who runs away from the self know the self? That is why I say: Don't escape, instead wake up; don't change, instead see – because one who wakes up and sees himself finds religion coming to his door."

23   Ego: The Pinnacle of Religion

A rich man gave a party for his friends to mark a special occasion. The king of that state was also at the party, so the rich man's joy knew no bounds.

But hardly had the guests started on their feast that his happiness turned to anger. One of his slaves dropped a plate full of hot food onto his foot, and burned it. Anger flashed in his eyes. For sure, the slave had no chance of living for much longer! He started trembling with fear. But a drowning man will catch at any straw; he quoted a saying from the holy scripture of that country: "He who controls his anger goes to heaven."

His master heard it. Although his eyes were full of anger, yet he controlled himself and said, "I am not angry." On hearing this, the guests naturally started clapping and even the king praised him. The anger in the rich man's eyes turned into egoistic pride. He felt very elated.

But then the slave spoke again, "Heaven is for the one who forgives…"

His master said, "I forgive you."

Although how can there be forgiveness in eyes that are full of ego? But ego can also feed on forgiveness. The ways of the ego are very subtle.

That rich man now appeared to be very religious to his guests. They had always known him as a very harsh exploiter. Seeing this new side of him, they were struck with wonder. The king, sitting at the front, also looked at him as if he was looking at a person who was superior to him. The rich man no longer belonged to this earth; his head was touching the sky.

Finally, the slave completed the unfinished saying of the scripture: "...because God loves those who are compassionate."

The rich man looked around. Worldly greed had always been in his eyes, today it had become otherworldly, and he said to the slave, "Go, I free you. Now you are no longer my slave." And he also gave him a bag full of gold coins.

The anger in his eyes had turned into ego, and that ego had turned into greed.

Anger, greed, hatred, fear – are they not all manifestations that come from the same source?

And if religion is so cheap, what rich man wouldn't like to buy it?

Isn't religion also resting on pillars of fear and greed?

So I ask you: Then what are the pillars of irreligion? If ego is the spire of the temple of religion, then what will be the spire of the temple of *irreligion*?

24   The Gold Within

I was staying in a multimillionaire's house. What did he not have? But his eyes were very weak, and it was impossible not to feel moved when you saw them. He was busy getting richer from morning till night. His life was spent counting money, taking care of it and keeping it safe, but he was not rich. He was perhaps just a caretaker. Throughout the day he could earn, and at night he would guard. For the same reason, he could not even sleep. Which guardian of wealth has ever slept? Sleep, dreamless sleep, is the wealth of only those who become free from the madness of all types of wealth – of money, of fame, of religion. The one who is running in any kind of race spends his days and nights without any peace. Peacelessness lurks in the shadow of a running mind.

When the mind rests, there is peace.

At night, as I took my leave from that poor – but multimillionaire – host in order to go to bed, he said, "I also want to sleep. But sleep will not even look at me. My nights pass in cares and concerns. I can't believe what sorts of irrelevant thoughts keep running in my head. I can't believe the number of things that keep frightening me. Kindly tell me the way to a healthy and peaceful sleep. What should I do? I am going mad."

What method could I suggest to him? I knew his disease: it was wealth. Wealth was playing with him during the day and tormenting him through the night. The night is only a reaction to the day, the outcome of it.

Whatever the trouble may be, the fact is that the root cause of that trouble is the search for some kind of safety outside the self. Such a search will not provide any safety and will only increase the disease. And even after giving up all attempts to find safety and security, as long as a person does not come back to himself, his whole life will remain a long and painful dream. Real safety does not exist except within the self. But to find it, the courage to remain unsafe in all respects is essential.

I told the man a story, and then said, "Go and sleep" – and surprisingly he did.

The next day he had tears of gratitude and happiness in his eyes. Today, when I think about it, I can hardly believe it myself. What magic did that story work on him? Perhaps in some particular state of mind even an ordinary thing becomes extraordinary. Something of that sort must have happened. Possibly the arrow unintentionally struck the right spot. That night he did sleep, it is true. And thereafter new flowers started blossoming in his life.

What was that story? Naturally enough, the desire to know it has become deep in your eyes.

There was a great city. A saint came to visit it. Saints come and go, but there was something unusual about this one. Thousands of people were coming to his hut, and whoever came near it would return with the same fragrance and freshness that is found when digging below rocky waterfalls, or in the utter silence of the forest, or under the stars of the night sky.

The saint's name was also unusual: Koti Karna Shrone. He had been very rich before taking up sannyas and used to wear rings worth ten million rupees in his ears. That is why his name had become Koti Karna – "ears of ten million." He had had money, but when he did not find his inner poverty disappearing, he became rich by renouncing that wealth. He used to say the same thing to others; and, the music arising from his breath was his witness, the peace flowing from his eyes was his witness; the happiness showering from his words and his silences was his witness. If the mind is mature then freedom from wealth, fame, status and ambition becomes very easy. They are, after all, the games of children.

Thousands of people had collected outside the town to see and hear this saint, Shrone. Listening to him, their minds calmed down, like the flickering of a candle flame in a windless spot. In that crowd there was also a nun whose name was Katiyani. When the evening approached, she asked her attendant, "Go back and light the lamps in my house. I will not get up and leave these words of nectar."

When her servant reached the house, she found that it had been burgled. The thieves were collecting their booty inside, and their leader was outside, guarding the house.

She returned to Katiyani immediately. The thieves' leader followed her. She approached Katiyani and told her in a nervous voice, "Mistress, there are thieves in the house." But Katiyani did not pay any attention to her. She was lost in some other world, she kept listening to what she was hearing, she kept looking at what she was seeing, and kept sitting where she was sitting. She was in another world. Tears of love were flowing from her eyes. The servant became nervous and shook her, saying, "Mother, mother! Thieves have burgled the house. They are taking away all your gold ornaments."

Katiyani opened her eyes and said, "Oh mad one, don't be bothered; don't worry. Let them take what they want to take. All those clothes and ornaments are unreal. Because I was living in ignorance they looked real. The day the thieves' eyes open, they will also discover that they are unreal. As soon as your eyes open, you find the real gold that can neither be stolen nor taken away. I am looking at that gold. That gold is within the self."

Her servant could not understand anything. She was at a loss, she was speechless. What had happened to her mistress? But the heart of the thieves' leader was moved as if some door had opened within him, as if some unlighted lamp had become aflame in his soul. He went back and told his friends, "Friends, leave these bundles here. All these gold ornaments are unreal. Come with me. Let us also search for the same wealth that the mistress of this house has found and which has led her to discover that gold ornaments are unreal. I have also been looking for that same gold. It is not far away. It is close by. It is within the self."

25   The Way to Peace

After studying all the scriptures, Kach, the son of sage Brihaspati returned to his father's house. Whatever could be known, he knew it! But his mind had no peace; the desire for pleasures was agitating him; he was restless with the heat of pride. He had only gone in search of knowledge in order to get rid of all this, but the restlessness was still there, and in addition, the weight of his knowledge had increased it.

This is what happens. What link is there between a knowledge of the scriptures and the birth of peace? There is no direct link between them. On the contrary, that type of knowledge intensifies the ego and opens the half-opened gates of restlessness fully.

But is it right to call it knowledge if it cannot provide peace? Real knowledge, knowing, provides peace and lightness. Can that which creates restlessness and heaviness also be knowledge?

Ignorance is pain. But if knowledge is also pain then where is happiness found? If knowledge does not provide peace, then perhaps it will be impossible to find it. If peace cannot be found at the door of truth then where can it be found? Is there no truth in the scriptures?

All these questions were rising in Kach's mind like a storm. He was very worried. He said to his father, "I have read all the scriptures.

Whatever could be learned from my teacher, I have learned. But I have not found peace in all of this. I am very worried and restless. Now, kindly show me the way to peace. What shall I do to find peace?"

His observation was correct. Peace is not found – nor can it be found – in the scriptures; nor can any teacher give it to you. It is not a thing which can be found on the outside. In fact, there is no other way to discover it except through the self.

What did Brihaspati say to Kach? He said, "Peace can be found in renunciation."

Kach's desire for truth was not mere curiosity. It was the deepest desire of his life. So he gave up everything. He went totally into renunciation. He spent years of his life with just one loincloth. He performed penances with fasts and all kinds of bodily suppressions.

Years went by. But he could not hear the footsteps of peace approaching him. Then he gave up his loincloth as well. He started living stark naked. He thought that perhaps his attachment to his loincloth had been standing in his way. His renunciation was now undoubtedly complete, but peace was still unknown to him.

Eventually, he made the final preparation. He thought that perhaps the body itself was the last obstacle, that it represented a desire to hold on. But the truth of the matter was that penance and steadfastness had dried up his body and it was by now it was only there in name. Even so, it was still there. He decided to end it. He lit a fire and prepared himself to give up his body. Whatever the cost, he must find peace. To attain it, he was prepared to embrace even death. When the firewood started burning fiercely he went to seek his father's permission to jump into the fire. But Brihaspati laughingly stopped him and said, "O mad one! What will you gain by renouncing the body?

As long as the mind is full of desires, and it has been attached to them for so long, nothing will be gained by burning the body. Desire always takes on new bodies and ego finds new homes. That is why renunciation of the body is no renunciation. Renunciation of the mind is true renunciation, and in renunciation of the mind lies peace, because freedom from the mind is peace."

For some moments Kach was speechless. Like a person who does not know what to do, he asked, "But how is the renunciation of the mind possible?"

Perhaps you are also asking me the same question. Whoever is in search of peace faces this basic difficulty. Whoever is engaged in the search for truth and salvation has this question. The mind itself is the barrier. The mind itself is restlessness.

What is this mind? Is not the desire to be something the mind? For a moment, please come out of your sleep and see this truth. Isn't the desire to be something, the race to be something, the thirst to be something, the very mind itself?

If there is no thirst to be anything then where is the mind? If, even for a moment, I am there, I am what I am, and there is no desire in me to be anything other than that, then where is the mind? And if this is true, how can the mind itself search out peace and truth? It is the mind that is in search of peace, so desire is also there. What then is it that wants to be peaceful? What is it that wants to find the truth? What is it that is desirous of salvation? Is it not the mind itself? And if all this is the mind, then how can we be free from it?

In fact, renunciation of the mind cannot be achieved by any attempt or effort of the mind itself, because any attempt from the mind will ultimately strengthen and give power to it – and will do so. Any of the mind's actions is just a follow-up and search for its own desires. As a result, it is only natural that it will be fed by its actions and become stronger.

That is why it is impossible to be free from the mind through any action of the mind itself. How can the mind be responsible for its own death? It thrives in worldly desires, but it also finds life in the desire for salvation. The same thing that exists in the world exists in religion. Being unsuccessful in the world, disappointed, and getting bored, the same mind which wants the world and its pleasures starts wishing for peace, wishing for truth. The mind is the same because basically the desire is the same.

Where there is desire there is mind. Desire is the world, desire is also renunciation. All renunciations, all giving up of the world, are born out of desire. All these are reactions to indulgence – and as long as there is some reaction there is no freedom. Whenever an action is a reaction to something, it is tied to it, is born out of it. It is another form of it; it is the same.

Renunciation is also an indulgence. Renunciation is the world itself. Whether it is indulgence or renunciation, the world or sannyas, the original form of mind – the central concentration of the mind – remains undisturbed in both. The life of the mind is desire. The thirst for being something, for getting something, for reaching somewhere is its very foundation stone. That is why peace is found neither in indulgence nor in renunciation.

Peace is there, and only there, when the mind is absent. The presence of mind means restlessness. The absence of mind is peace. Where mind does not exist, exists that which is real. But you will ask, "How can it happen?" My friends, do not ask, because it is the mind that is asking. The search for "How?" belongs to the mind. The search for ways and means belongs to the mind. The search for being something belongs to the mind. It always asks "How?"

No. Do not ask this, but observe what the ways of the mind are. Through what means does it get integrated? By what methods does it become improved? By what methods does it become powerful? Surely, its ways are very subtle. Wake up to these ways. Do nothing, but simply stay awake. Be watchful and alert to its forms and sub-forms. Understand the mind. Recognize it in its totality. Be awake to its actions and reactions, its attachments and detachments, its likes and dislikes. Let it be remembered every moment. Let it not be forgotten. Attention to it has to be natural. Our eyes must be automatically on it. A revolution will only come about through understanding and getting to know it without any tension or concentration. In fact, knowing this is the revolution.

In knowing the mind, the mind itself disappears. In learning to recognize it, it drops, because knowing and being aware of something are not desires. They are not racing to be, or not be, something. This is merely a wakefulness towards that which exists and that which is happening. Desire is always for the future, knowing is always for the present. That is why the advent of knowing becomes the farewell to desire. Knowing the mind is freedom from the mind.

Remember that this is not the freedom of the mind, it is freedom from the mind itself, and in this boundless light of freedom godliness is known.

Knowing Each Other 26

From morning till night, I see hundreds of people indulging in slandering one another. How quickly we decide about others! In fact, nothing is more difficult than deciding about someone else. Perhaps no one, except God, has a right to pass judgment on others, because who else, other than God, possesses the necessary patience to judge a person, a small and very ordinary person?

Do we know each other? Even those who are very close, do they really know each other? Don't even friends continue to be unknown to each other and strangers?

But we claim to understand even the unknown and take decisions so quickly about others!

This haste is extremely ugly. But the person who keeps on thinking about others totally forgets to think about the self. Such haste is utter ignorance because with knowledge comes patience. Life is very mysterious, and those who get into the habit of taking hasty decisions without thinking properly fail to understand this.

I have heard a story. It relates to the First World War.

A commander told his soldiers, "Men, five of you are required for a very dangerous mission. Therefore, those of you who are prepared to take the risk voluntarily take two steps out of the line."

He had just finished talking when someone riding a horse came by and diverted his attention. He had come to deliver a really important message to the commander. After reading the message, the commander lifted his eyes towards the soldiers of his unit. Finding their lines intact, he was enraged. His eyes started burning and he cried out, "You cowards, you weaklings! Is there not even one man amongst you all?" He hurled many other abuses at them, and threatened to punish them.

Only then did he observe that not only one, but all the soldiers had come forward, out of the line, by two steps!

Swimming with Existence 27

One day, I sat down by the side of a road. Sitting under the ample shade of a tree I started looking at the passers-by.

Seeing them, several thoughts crossed my mind. They were all running somewhere – children, young, old, women, men – they were all running away. Their eyes seemed to be searching for something and their feet were busy on some long journey. But where were they running to? What was their purpose and would they, in the end, know that they had reached somewhere?

The same thought arises in me when I see you.

When I have this thought I am touched by severe pain because I know that you will not reach anywhere. You will not reach, because your minds and feet are running in the opposite direction from existence.

The secret of reaching somewhere in life is to move in the direction of existence. Except that, no direction, no road, leads anywhere. Swim in the direction of existence. Swimming against it, a person only falls apart and destroys himself.

What is man's fear? What is his concern? What is his pain? What is his death? I have seen that all our troubles come in the wake of our vain attempts to swim against the flow of existence. Ego is pain, ego is a disease – because ego goes in the opposite direction to existence, and opposition to existence is opposition to the self.

I have heard a story…

The pilot of a small aircraft was flying at a speed of one hundred and fifty miles an hour. Suddenly, he found himself in a deadly current of wind. It was very stormy. It is possible that it was also moving at the speed of one hundred and fifty miles per hour but in the opposite direction to the plane. The pilot's life, caught up as he was in the fierce storm, was in danger, and it seemed impossible that his plane would land safely. The strange thing was that all the parts of his plane were working as normal and the engines were making a loud noise, and yet the plane was not moving even an inch.

Afterwards, the pilot said, "How strange that experience was; not to move at all even while flying at the speed of a hundred and fifty miles per hour! I was going so fast and yet I was going nowhere!"

Is it not also true that moving against oneself one cannot reach anywhere? Happiness in life belongs to those who live in the self, know the self, and attain the self.

Is this not also true in life, is this not also happening there – that those who are not moving in the same direction as existence will find that they are without a doubt moving, yet not reaching anywhere?

Godliness is the internal existence of the self; existence is the very form of the self.

Emperors, Not Slaves 28

Friends, what do I teach? I teach a small secret. I teach the secret of becoming an emperor in the world. What could be a bigger secret than this small one?

You may ask how everyone in the world can become an emperor. I say that it can be; there is a large empire where everyone is an emperor. But, everyone that we know in the world is merely a slave. Even those who are under the illusion of thinking that they are emperors are just slaves.

Just as there is a world outside man, there is also a world inside him. In the outer world nobody has ever been an emperor, although most people have struggled only to become one.

Perhaps you are also in that same struggle, in that same competition? But he who wants to become an emperor, that is, to rule not the world but the self...

Jesus has said, "The kingdom of God is within you."

Don't you know that those who have conquered kingdoms on the outside have lost the self? And how can one who loses himself become an emperor? To be an emperor, it is at least imperative to know the self. No! No! The external world takes you deeply into poverty. In that world those who look like emperors are the slaves of their own slaves.

Desires, thirsts and ambitions do not allow freedom. On the contrary, they tie you down in the most imperceptible and yet the strongest of bonds. No chains have ever been made – or can ever be made in the future – that are stronger than the chains of desires. In fact no steel has ever been made so strong. How can a person bound in these invisible chains ever become an emperor?

There was a king: Frederick the Great of Prussia. One evening, outside the capital, he was bumped into by an elderly man. The path was narrow and the darkness of the evening was encroaching on all sides. In anger, Frederic asked that old man, "Who are you?"

The old man replied, "An emperor."

Frederic asked in amazement, "An emperor?" and then he threw a jibe: "Which kingdom do you rule?"

That old man replied, "My own being."

Surely, those who rule the self are indeed emperors.

Indifference towards Religion 29

Why this indifference towards religion? And why is it increasing every day?

I have heard a story…

There was a village. The residents there were very simple. Whatever anybody told them, they would accept.

Outside their village there stood a statue of their god. A saint came to the village, gathered all the villagers together there and said, "This is very bad, very bad! You fools: you live in the shade and yet your god is out in the sun? Put a roof over your god. Don't you see how angry he is?"

The villagers were very poor, but somehow, by reducing their own roofs, they managed to make a roof for their god. Once the roof had gone up the saint left for another village. He had charge of not only one village, but many. There were many gods, and he had taken on the responsibility of providing shelter for them all.

Then, after a few days, another saint came to the village. He was distraught when he saw the roof over their god. He collected the village people together and showed them his temper. He said, "This is very bad. You fools! Why have you put a roof over your god? Does he need your cover? If there is a fire, he will be all burned up. Take it off and throw it away, quickly!"

The villagers were surprised. But what else could they do? Whatever the saints say is always correct, and if you do not accept their words, then they can trouble you with a curse that will last for several lives or make you rot in hell. God is in their hands, and therefore, whatever they want gets done.

Those poor people had to take off the roof and throw it away. The labor of so many days, the energy and the resources of these poor people were all wasted. But surely whatever had happened was a piece of luck because they had been saved from the shame of putting a roof over their god! After they had taken away the roof the saint went away to another village. After all, he had not only one village to look after, but several. There were many gods, and it was his responsibility to keep all of them free from any covering.

But soon another saint came to the village. By that time the villagers were fully aware and they would not walk in the direction of their god's statue even by mistake. They did not know what other troubles might be created. They had stopped going that way at all.

I have found that what happened in that village has happened in the world at large. Saints have done such ugly things and established such fears in the minds of people – all in the name of religion – that it is no wonder that people have stopped going in the direction of God.

Indifference to religion is ultimately indifference to the fears and blind faiths spread by those so-called saints.

Indifference to religion is indifference to the exploitation, hypocrisy and foolishness that come in the garb of religion.

Indifference to religion is indifference to all those sects which have become false substitutes for religion.

Indifference to religion is indifference to the hate, jealousies and enmity created by them.

Indifference to religion is not indifference to it, but is, in fact, indifference to all that which is not religion.

30   Find the Problem First

A king's prime minister had died, so the king had before him the difficult problem of finding the most intelligent person in the land and making him the new prime minister. After several kinds of tests, three people were finally selected. Out of those three one still had to be chosen.

One day, before the final selection test, a rumor went around that the monarch was going to shut the candidates in a room, on the door of which a wonderful lock, prepared by the best mechanics of the land, would be fixed, and that this lock would only be able to be opened by a person who was very good at mathematics. Out of those three candidates, two could not sleep that night for worry and excitement. Throughout the night they kept studying books on locks and trying to memorize the numbers and mathematical formulae.

Even before the day had dawned, they were so stuffed with arithmetic that it was almost impossible for them to add two and two. On their way to the palace, they concealed a few books on mathematics under their clothes that might at some point be needed. In their own eyes they were fully prepared, although because they has stayed awake with their books throughout the night their minds were not sharp and their feet were stumbling as if they were drunk. Treatises and knowledge have their own intoxication. But to both of them, the third man who had slept very peacefully the night before appeared to be crazy. What else could his carefree ways indicate but that? Both of them had been laughing, and were still laughing, at his foolishness.

As soon as they reached the palace they came to believe that all the rumors they had heard were certainly true. They were immediately shut into a big room on the door of which the much talked-about lock was fixed. For its time, the lock was a superb invention of mechanical intelligence. It had been constructed on a mathematical basis and was like a very challenging puzzle which could only be solved mathematically. They had known about all these things through rumors, and the arithmetical figures and marks made on the lock seemed to prove this.

Once they had been shut in the room the three men came to know that whoever opened the lock and was able to come out first would be appointed to the position of prime minister by the king. The two who had been studying all night immediately started reading the marks on the lock and doing arithmetical calculations. In between, they also consulted the books that they had brought with them. It was winter and from the big windows in the room a cold morning wind was blowing in, but their foreheads were perspiring. Time was short, the problem of opening the lock was difficult, and in a short while their lives' future was to be decided. Their hands were trembling and their breathing was fast. They were writing one thing and calculating something else.

But the one of them who had slept throughout the night neither studied the lock, nor lifted his pen, nor tried to solve any mathematical problems. He just sat patiently with his eyes shut. His face showed neither any worry nor any excitement. On looking at him one could not feel that he was thinking about anything. His wholeness and presence looked like the steady flame of a lamp in a room in which there is no wind. He was absolutely calm, silent, and blank. But then, suddenly, he got up and appearing extremely natural and calm he moved slowly to the door of the room. Then very slowly he turned the handle of the door and, surprisingly, the door fell open.

The lock and the whole story connected with it had been a deception. But his two friends who were busy solving mathematical problems knew nothing about this. They did not even know that one of them was no longer in the room. This astonishing fact became known to them only when the king himself came into the room and said, "Gentlemen, now stop this mathematics! The person who deserved to get out has already done so."

Those poor fellows were not able to believe their eyes. Their friend, who was undeserving in all respects, was standing behind the king. Finding them lost for words, the king said to them, "In life, this is of primary importance: we should first of all find out whether a problem really exists or not, whether the lock is actually locked or not. The person who does not identify the problem and gets involved in solving it is, naturally, misled and is misdirected forever."

This story is strangely true.

I have found the same thing even in relation to God. His door has also been open since the beginning of time and all rumors about the locks on that door are absolutely untrue. But the anxious candidates wanting to enter his gates carry their scriptures with them out of a fear of those locks. Then these scriptures and teachings themselves become locks for them. They remain sitting outside the door. How can they enter through the door unless they have solved the mathematical problems through their scriptures? Rarely does someone muster the courage to reach the door without some scriptures.

I reached like that, and on reaching I found that, as far as the eyes could see, the learned ones sat buried under piles of their own scriptures and were so engrossed in solving problems that they could not even sense the arrival of a person as undeserving as I was. I reached and turned the handle of the door and found that it was already open. At first, I felt that it was my luck, that the doorkeepers may have made some mistake. Otherwise, how could it be possible that a person who knew no scriptures and had no learning would gain entrance to the world of truth? I entered fearfully, but those who were already inside told me that the rumor about the closure of the door to God was spread by the Devil and was a rumor with absolutely no basis to it because his doors were always open.

Can't the doors of love also be closed like that? Can't the doors of truth also be closed like that?

31   Death Is Hidden within Birth

It is very surprising that man accepts birth but not death, when birth and death are but two ends of the same occurrence.

Death is hidden within birth – because isn't birth just the beginning of death? From then onwards, resisting death leads to fear, and out of fear, running away. The fearful and escaping mind becomes unable to understand death. But however much you may run, it is impossible to run away from death, because it has been present since birth. It is not possible to run away from death; on the contrary, after running in all directions, in the end you discover that only death has been reached.

There is an old story…

Vishnu went to Mount Kailash to meet Shiva. He was flown there by Garuda, the king of all feathered beings. After Vishnu dismounted, Garuda waited for him at the gate. While he was there his eyes fell upon a pigeon, trembling with fear, and sitting on the top of the door. He asked him what he was frightened of. The pigeon started weeping and said, "Just recently the God of Death entered his palace. On seeing me, he faltered for a while, looked at me in surprise, and then, with a smile, went ahead moving his club around. His mysterious smile is nothing but a sure indication of my death. My end is near." And the pigeon started weeping even more loudly.

Garuda replied, "Tut! tut! You are unnecessarily so afraid. You are still young and therefore there is no possibility of your dying because of some disease. And as far as fearing any enemy is concerned, come and sit on my back. In an instant, I will take you to Lokalok Hill which is thousands of millions of miles away from here. There will be no chance of any of your enemies being there."

On hearing this solution the pigeon felt better, and in an instant Garuda had taken him to the lonely hill where he could move around away from any enemies. But as soon as Garuda returned he met the God of Death coming out of the gate. Garuda smiled and said, "Sir, that pigeon is no longer here. He is living without fear on Lokalok Hill, which is thousands of millions of miles away. I have just returned from leaving him there."

On hearing this, the God of Death laughed loudly and said, "So it is you who have finally taken him there? I was only surprised, wondering how he got there. He will have entered the jaws of death within a few moments of arriving on there."

32   The Person Who Decides to Give Up
Never Does So

A young man came to me. He was ready to renounce the world, and soon after making all the necessary preparations he was to take sannyas. He was very happy because his preparations were almost complete.

When I heard what he had to say I started laughing and said to him, "I have heard about preparations for the world. What is this about preparation for renunciation? Is it necessary to make preparations and to plan even for renunciation? And will this renunciation, which is so well planned, ever be a renunciation at all? Isn't it an extension of the worldly mind?"

"The world and renunciation cannot co-exist in the same mind. A worldly mind can never be a renouncing mind. The switch from the world to renunciation cannot take place without a fundamental revolution in the mind. This basic revolution is itself renunciation. Sannyas is neither a change of dress, nor a change of name, nor a change of house. It is a change of outlook; it is a total change of the mind, of the self. For that revolution, the same processes which are successful in the world do not work. The arithmetic of the world is not only useless but even an obstruction for that revolution. Just as the rules in dreams do not work while awake, similarly the truths of the world do not continue to be truths in sannyas. After all, sannyas is waking up from the world of dreams."

Then I stopped, and looked at the young man. He looked somewhat pained. Perhaps I had given a jolt to his preparations and he had come to me with other expectations. Without saying anything, he began to turn away, so then I said to him, "Listen, hear one more story..."

There was a saint called Ajar Kaiwan. A man came to him at midnight and said, "Blessed One, I have taken a vow that I will give up all the pleasures of this mortal world. I have resolved to break all ties with this world."

If I had been there I would have told him, "Oh you fool, he who takes an oath is a weak man and he who decides to renounce never does so. And even if he does renounce, he clings to the fact he has 'given up.' Renunciation is not a resolve of the ignorant mind. It is a natural part of knowledge."

But I was not there, Kaiwan was. He said to that person, "You have thought rightly."

The man was pleased and went away. He returned after some days and said, "At the moment I am preparing a mattress and my clothes. As soon as I have collected my things together I will become a monk."

But this time even Kaiwan could not say that he was thinking correctly. He said, "Friend, it is only by giving up accumulating that someone becomes a monk and you are worried about accumulating! Go away, go back to your world. You are not yet in a position to renounce."

33   A Life of Love, a Life of Prayerfulness

When I see you going to the temples to worship God, I start wondering whether God only exists in temples, because outside the temples, there is neither the sparkle of innocence in your eyes nor the sound of prayers on your breath. Outside the temples you are just like those people who have never been to them. Doesn't this prove the futility of going to the temples? Is it possible that outside, on the temple steps, you can be harsh, and yet inside, compassionate? Is it believable that cruel minds will immediately become full of love on entering the temple doors? How can prayers to God be born in those hearts that have no love for the universe?

The one whose very life is not love cannot have prayer in his life. And the one who cannot see the divine in every atom will not find godliness anywhere.

It happened at night. An unknown traveler reached the temple of Mecca very tired and went to sleep. Finding his un-pious feet facing the holy stone of Kaaba, the priests lost their tempers. They dragged him out of his sleep and said, "What sin you have committed! What temerity, to insult the holy stone of the temple in this manner! Is this the way to sleep? Surely, only an atheist can point his feet towards the temple of God!"

Even after having observed their angry gestures and hearing their insulting and harsh words the traveler started laughing and he said, "All right, I will place my feet wherever God does not exist. Please be kind enough to put my feet in such a direction. As far as I am concerned, I find his temple on all sides and in all directions."

This strange traveler was Nanak. How true his reply is: "Surely God exists everywhere? But I want to ask you whether he does not also exist in your feet? He is there. What else is there except him? Existence? – he is the whole existence. But the eyes that see him only in temples, statues, and holy rivers often become dazed when they see him in his fullness."

34   Accept Yourself

One day I was in a forest. It was the rainy season and the trees were full of joy. I asked my companions, "Do you see how happy the trees are? And why? – because they have become what they actually were meant to be. If the seed is one thing and the tree wishes to become something else, there will not be so much happiness in the forest, but because the trees know nothing about ideals, they have become what their nature wanted them to be. Fulfillment lies where what unfolds is in keeping with something's own form and self-nature. Man is in misery because he is against himself. He fights with his own roots and is constantly struggling to be different from what he is. In this way he loses himself and also loses that paradise which is his natural right."

Friends, is it not desirable to wish to be what you can be? Is it not desirable for you to give up all efforts to be anything other than your own selves? Is it not in that very desire that the main source of all miseries lives? What attempt could be more impossible and meaningless than the desire to be different from yourself? Everyone can be only that which he can be: in the seed is hidden the development of a tree. The desire to be something else can only lead to failure – failure, because how can that which is not hidden in the self from the beginning manifest in the end?

Life is a manifestation of that which is covered and hidden at birth. Development, growth, is simply its uncovering, and when the hidden does not manifest, there is misery. Just as a mother will find herself in unbearable and indescribable pain if she carries the child in her womb for her whole life, similarly those people who do not become what they were destined to be find they are miserable. But I observe that every person is running in the same race. Everyone wants to be what he is not and so no one can ever succeed. What is the ultimate result? The result is that people do not become what they could have been. And as they do not become what they cannot be, they are also deprived of what they dreamed they could become.

The king of a tribe went to a big city for the first time. He wanted to get himself photographed. He was taken to a studio. The photographer had a board on his gate on which was written: "Have yourself photographed however you like. Just as you are: 10 rupees. As you think you are: 15 rupees. How you want to present yourself to others: 20 rupees. As you wish you could have been: 25 rupees."

That simple king was very surprised by all of this and inquired if people other than those wanting to have the first type of photograph came. He was told that a person wanting to have the first type of photograph had not yet appeared in the shop.

May I ask what type of photograph you would have liked to get from that photographer? What does your mind say? Deep down, wouldn't you have liked the last type of photograph? It is something different if you don't have enough money with you, the pressure of circumstances may make a difference, but otherwise, who would like to have the first type of photograph? But that "fool" of a king did get himself photographed as the first type, and said, "I have come here to get a photograph of myself and not of someone else."

A similar board has been hanging all the time on the door of life. God hung it there, well before he made man.

All hypocrisy in this world is born out of the desire to be different from the self. When someone fails to be anything other than what he is, he busies himself with *appearing* to be different. Isn't this what we call hypocrisy? And if a person fails even in this attempt he becomes disturbed. Then he feels free to imagine himself in whatever way he wants to. But whether it is hypocrisy or madness, the origin of either lies in refusing to accept oneself.

The first symptom of a healthy person is his acceptance of the self. He has been born into life for a picture of himself to be made, and not of someone he is not. All attempts to mold oneself into the frames of others are indications of a diseased mind. The so-called ideals taught to man, and the inspirations given to him to follow others do not allow him to accept himself – and then his journey will take a wrong turning from the very beginning.

But this type of "civilization" has grasped man just like a chronic disease would do. How ugly and deformed people have become! There is nothing healthy or natural in them. Why? Because in the name of culture, civilization and education, their very nature has been persistently murdered. If man does not become alert to this conspiracy, then he will be destroyed right down to his very roots.

Culture is not opposed to nature; it is the growth of it. The future of man can be determined not by any external ideals but by his intrinsic nature. Then an inner discipline is born which is so natural and which opens and uncovers the face of one's self to such an extent that the ultimate truth can be seen.

That is why I say, choose yourself, accept yourself, search and develop yourself. Other than being your own self, there is no ideal for anyone; there can be none. Imitation is suicide. And remember that godliness can never be found by depending on others.

35   Our Own Reflections in Others

Early in the morning a friend came to see me. His eyes were burning with anger and hatred. He was uttering very harsh, poisonous, and hot words about someone. I patiently heard him out and then asked whether he had heard about an incident. He was in no mood to listen to anything, but even so he asked, "What incident?"

When I started laughing, he became a little more relaxed. Then I told him...

A psychologist was doing some research on love and hatred. He told a class of fifteen students in a university that they should write down, within thirty seconds, the initials of the names of any of the other young men whom they might consider deserved to be hated.

One young man could not write down the name of anybody; others wrote a few names. One wrote down the maximum number of names. The findings of this experiment were very surprising. The young men who had mentioned the largest number of names of people that they hated, were themselves the most hated by others, and the most wonderful and meaningful thing was that the name of the person who had written no names down, was not written down by anybody.

Those whom a person meets on the path of life very often prove to be a mirror. Don't we find our own reflection in others? If you have hatred in you, you will find others worthy of that hatred. That hatred creates and invents the hateful by itself. And these creations and inventions have a purpose: in this way a person is saved the trouble of seeing what is hateful inside himself. When you make a mountain out of a molehill and see it in others, then what seems like a mountain in you starts looking more like a molehill.

There are only two ways of escaping the pain of being able to see with only one eye: either you cure your eye, or you imagine that others have lost both theirs. Surely the latter way seems easier, because in that way nothing has to be done; it is enough just to imagine.

Let us remember that when we meet others, we should consider them to be a mirror and whatever we see in them we should first of all search for in ourselves. In this way, in the mirror of day-to-day interactions, a person becomes busy searching for his own self.

Running away from the world and its interactions is not only cowardly but also useless. The right thing is to use those interactions in a search for the self. Without them, it is as impossible to find out about oneself as it is to see one's own face without a mirror. In the form of others, we constantly keep meeting our own selves. The heart, which is full of love, sees love in all others. Ultimately the culmination of this experience brings you face-to-face with the divine.

On this earth there are people who live in hell and people who live in heaven. The main source of pain and pleasure, hell and heaven, is within us, and whatever is within us is thrown up onto the outer screen. It is the eyes of man that see nothing but death among the things of this world; it is again the eyes of man which observe the eternal beauty and music of the divine in this universe.

Therefore, that which appears on the outside is not the eternal or the core of life but what is inside us. Those who have their eyes constantly on this truth become free from outer things and become settled in their interiority. Those who keep this mainspring in mind in pleasure and pain, in hatred and love, with friend and enemy, find that ultimately there is neither pleasure nor pain, neither enemy nor friend, only the self: I am my own enemy, and I am my own friend.

Echoes

Echoes 36

I was in the hills. A few friends were with me. One day, we went to a valley where the hills produced very clear echoes. A friend made the sound of a dog and dogs started barking in the hills. Then someone made the sound of the *kokil* and the valley started resounding with a sweet "Ku-hu, ku-hu."

I said to them, "The world is also like this. Whatever we throw out is returned to us. Flowers beget flowers and thorns beget thorns. For a heart full of love, the entire world starts showering love, and for a person full of hatred, painful flames of fire start burning everywhere."

Then I told a story to those friends…

A young boy went into the forest near his village for the first time. He was very afraid and wary of loneliness. Just then, he heard some creeping sound in the bushes. Surely, somebody was secretly following him? He shouted out loudly, asking, "Who is there?"

The hills replied a little more loudly, "Who is there?"

By then he was fully convinced that someone was hiding from him. He was even more afraid. His hands and feet started trembling, and his heart started pounding. But to give himself courage, he shouted at the hidden person, "You coward!" Then there was the echo: "You coward!" For the last time he gathered his nerve and shouted back, "I will kill you!" The hills and the forest shouted back, "I will kill you!"

The boy ran quickly back to the village. The echo of his own feet sounded like the other person chasing him, but by now he did not have the courage even to turn back and look. On reaching the door of his house, he fell down unconscious. When he came back to his senses, the whole thing came out into the open. On hearing all about it, his mother laughed loudly and said, "Go there again tomorrow and tell that mysterious person what I tell you to. I know all about that person. He is a very nice and loveable man."

The boy went there the next day. On reaching the same place he said, "My friend!" There was the echo of "My friend!" This friendly sound consoled him and he said, "I love you!" The hills and the forest all repeated, "I love you!"

Isn't this story about the echo the story of our so-called lives? Aren't we all children and strangers in the forest of this world, who, on hearing our own echoes, become afraid and run? Are we not in the same situation?

Remember that if "I will kill you'" is an echo, so too is "I love you." Becoming free from the first echo and falling in love with the second is no escape from childhood. Some are afraid of the first echo and some start loving the second, but basically, there is no difference between the two. Immaturity is hidden in both.

The one who knows lives free from both illusions. The reality of life is not found in echoes; it is hidden within the self.

The World Is as Our Eyes See It 37

I had just woken from my sleep when I received the news that some-one in the neighborhood had been murdered. Everyone was busy talking about it. There was sensation in the air and the normally lusterless eyes of people were shining. No one felt either pain or sympathy; there was only a diseased and unsavory feeling around. Can death and murder also give pleasure? Can destruction also bring happiness? Maybe it is so, other-wise the general public's mind could not be so enthusiastic about wars.

When the current of life cannot move on the path of creativity then all of a sudden it gets involved with destruction; then, in order to mani-fest itself, the only alternative is destruction. The person who does not make himself creative changes the direction of his life to destruction in spite of himself. In individuals, in society, in nations, everywhere there is an eagerness for destruction.

Man's orientation towards destruction ultimately becomes suicidal. If the taste for destruction develops, ultimately it destroys the self. There is not much difference between the killer and the self-killer. At its most extreme, violence changes into violence against the self.

I knew the person who had been murdered that night, and I also knew the man who had murdered him. They were old enemies, and for years they had been looking for an opportunity to kill one another. Perhaps they had no other ambition in life except this major task. Perhaps, for that same reason, the murderer gave himself up into the hands of the law after committing the murder. What was the point of living now? The one for whom he had been living was no longer there.

Isn't it surprising that most of us live only for our enemies? Those who live and die for friends are very few. Not love but hatred has become the basis of life. Then it is only natural to find a hidden pleasure in death and our lives find a helpless eagerness for and attraction to destruction. It is not without reason that individuals are attracted to violence, and nations to wars.

What is this hatred? Is it not a revenge on others for not being able to take our own lives to the peaks of happiness? Surely it is so, because we make others responsible for what we cannot achieve ourselves, and so we find an easy and simple way out of feeling remorse for our own lives.

What is this enmity? Doesn't it advertise our own failure to be friendly? Does enmity end by finishing off the enemy? Enmity gives birth to the enemy. That is why the enemy can be destroyed, but the enmity will still remain. Can friendship be destroyed by the death of a friend? No? Then, how can enmity be destroyed by finishing off the enemy? The friend and the enemy are seen on the outside, but the origin is within oneself. The Ganges of life is outside, but the Gangotri, the source of the Ganges, is always within. I, for one, find in everyone the echo of myself. Whatever I am is reflected in others.

I am reminded of an incident...

It was a no-moon night. A man was about to enter someone's house and murder him. There was no one else around, but he was very afraid inside. There was silence all around, but within him there was a lot of noise and turbulence. Full of fear, and with trembling hands, he opened the door. It was surprising, the door was not locked from inside; it was just shut. But what was this? As soon as he opened the door, he saw a strong and cruel-looking man standing in front of him with a gun in his hand. Possibly, it was a watchman? But there was no way to go back. Death was standing in front of him. There was no time even to think. In self-defense he fired his gun.

All this happened within a split second. The entire house reverberated with the sound of the bullet, and something broke and shattered into pieces. What was it? The man who had fired the gun was stunned. There was no one in front of him, only the smoke from the bullet and a mirror that had shattered into pieces.

The same thing is also seen in life. In our imagined need for self-defense, we start fighting with mirrors. Because there is fear inside, the enemy starts appearing on the outside. Because death is inside, the murderer starts fearing the outside. But can enemies be removed by breaking mirrors? An enemy can be destroyed in friendship, but not by his death. Except love, everything else is a defeat.

The enemy lives within ourselves: in our hatred of ourselves, in our fear, enmity and jealousy of ourselves. But it starts appearing on the outside. There is yellowness in the eyes of a jaundiced person, but he sees the whole world as yellow. What is the right thing to do with such a disease? Should we eliminate the color yellow from the whole world or treat our own eyes?

The world is as our eyes see it. In our own eyes are hidden the colors of the enemy and the friend. Nobody wants an enemy, yet we keep cherishing enmity. Even from the desire to eliminate an enemy it is evident that we do not want the enemy but want a friend. But we nourish hatred in our blood. It is absolute foolishness. We want friends, but we do not give birth to love. We want friends but enemies are born instead. We murder our enemies but in doing so potential friends are murdered. We sow seeds of poison when we want fruits of nectar. This will not be possible.

Both friends and enemies are shadows of one's own self.

If I am love, the whole of the world is a friend.

If I am hatred, even existence is an enemy.

The Ways of the Ego 38

A friend sometimes comes to see me. Whenever I see him, I am always reminded of a saying of Socrates. Socrates said to a wandering monk, "My friend, out of your torn and beggarly clothes nothing but ego peeps out."

The ways of ego are very subtle. When it is covered with humility it is in its subtlest form. But rather than cover it, such humility reveals it more. It is like those clothes that do not really cover the body but only expose it. In fact, neither does the cover of love eliminate hatred nor do the clothes of humility cover the nakedness of ego. Just as coals are safely hidden beneath the ashes until the slightest puff of wind exposes them, similarly the truth remains hidden by individuals until the slightest tug on the curtain opens it and exposes everything. Such invisible diseases are much more dangerous and lethal than visible diseases, but man's skill at deceiving himself is very well-developed, and he uses this skill to such an extent that it has becomes his second nature.

Over thousands of years, in our attempts to bring civilization by force, nothing has been achieved except this skill. Man has succeeded not in destroying nature but in covering it, and in this way so-called civilization has proved itself to be a chronic disease.

How can civilization be born if it is opposed to nature? From that, not civilization but only non-civilization will flourish. True civilization is a beautiful exposition of nature. Self-deception cannot take a man anywhere. But compared to an inner revolution, self-deception is very easy, and every time we make the mistake of choosing the easier option. But the easier option is not always the best. How can you choose the easiness of going downhill when you want to touch the summits of the mountains of life?

It is very easy to deceive oneself. In deceiving others, there may be the fear of being caught; in deceiving oneself even that fear is absent. Those who deceive others suffer punishment and insults on this earth, and even in the other world the severe tortures of hell are waiting for them, but those who deceive themselves get respect in this world, and they also think they deserve heaven in the next. It is for this reason that man deceives himself without any fear. Otherwise, how could the whole hypocrisy of civilization and religion have been born?

But can you hide and destroy what is true? Can man succeed in deceiving the self, everyone else, and ultimately existence itself? Isn't all this effort sheer foolishness?

It is right to know the self as it is, because without accepting the reality of oneself there can be no real change in the self. Just as for the body to be healthy again it is necessary to know everything about a disease, similarly, for spiritual health it is necessary to know your inner diseases. It is not in the interests of a patient to cover up disease, but in the interests of the disease itself. For there to be any treatment, diagnosis is essential, so those who want to escape diagnosis will remain without treatment.

A sculptor was making a statue of Ralf Waldo Emerson. Every day, Emerson used to watch the development of his form out of the stone intently, and as the statue evolved, he became more and more serious.

At last, one day, when the statue was almost complete, Emerson became extremely grave. The sculptor asked him the reason for his seriousness, and he replied, "I observe that as the statue is becoming more like myself it is becoming more unshapely and ugly."

I consider this power to see oneself in all one's ugliness, nakedness, and animalism to be the first step on the ladder of self-revolution.

Only the person who is able to see the ugliness in himself is capable of giving beauty to himself. Without the capacity for the first, the second is not possible, and anyone who covers up his own ugliness and busies himself with forgetting it will remain ugly forever. To know and accept the Ravana, the evil, in oneself is the first, inevitable step to becoming a Rama, a virtuous person. The ugliness of life remains hidden and secure if one remains unconscious about it.

First of all, I will have to know myself as I am. There is no alternative. If, on this very first point of the journey, we give room to falsehood then the truth can never be found in the end. But because of its ugliness we disown the reality of the self and start nourishing an unreal and imaginary personality. This desire for beauty is all right in itself, but the path is not right. The ugliness of the self cannot be eliminated by putting on beautiful masks, and what is more, because of such masks the self continues to become even more ugly and unshapely. Then slowly, all knowledge of the self disappears, and we only remain acquainted with and recognize our false masks. If one's own face is lost it becomes impossible to recognize the self anymore.

A lady went to the bank to take out some money. The cashier asked her. "How do I know that you are who you say you are?"

She quickly took a mirror out from her bag, looked into it and said, "Believe me. I am who I say I am."

In your search for truth, in your search for the existence of your real self, first you will have to wrestle with your own masks. Without discovering your real face, you can neither discover yourself nor refine yourself. The palace of truth stands on the foundations of reality. And no other power except truth can bring civilization.

A Very Strange Contest   39

Last night, a young woman came to me and said, "I want to serve people."

I told her, "If you forget the 'I,' service will automatically follow."

What else except ego stands in the way of life becoming a service?

Ego demands service. In fact, it just wants everything and gives nothing. It is incapable of giving. Giving is not possible for it. Ego has always been a beggar. Therefore, it is impossible to find anyone more miserable and poorer than an egoist.

Only someone who is a king can serve. What can a person give when he has nothing inside him? Before giving, it is essential to have something.

What is service? Isn't love itself service? And love is born only in a consciousness where "I" is dead and buried.

In the death of "I," is the birth and life of love.

From the funeral pyre of "I," the seed of love germinates.

Those who are full of "I," are empty of love. "I" is the center of exploitation. Even its service will be an exploitation. Even in service, the same "I" prospers and finds strength. Is humanity unaware of the ego of servants? Even an exploiter's ego has a covering of humility, but a servant's humility is a sheer declaration of ego. Remember that love is not vocal and service is silent.

And also remember that love is its own appreciation and service is its own reward.

I am reminded of a very strange contest...

Two friends went to a teacher to learn painting. They were both very poor. They did not have even two sticks to rub together. Both of them decided that, to begin with, one of them would practice art and the other one would take a job and feed himself and the other, and later on, the first one would earn and the other one would learn.

One of them started painting with the teacher. Years came and passed by. It was a tough discipline. There was no question of time: with full attention, the young man was busy with his efforts. Slowly, he started becoming famous. In the world of art, his star rose. The name of that young man was Albrecht Dürer. But his friend was busy making an effort even more difficult than Dürer's own. He was digging pits and breaking stones; cutting wood and carrying loads. Slowly, slowly, he completely forgot that he too had come to learn painting, and when it was his turn to learn the art, it was observed that his hands had become so stiff, so hard and so unshapely that is was impossible to paint with them.

At this misfortune, the first young man started weeping, but the other one was very happy. He said, "What difference does it make whether it is your hand or mine that makes the pictures? Are your hands also not mine?"

The first young man became a great painter, but the name of his friend, who made him a painter through his sweat and toil, is not known to anyone. But isn't his unknown service a shining example of his love? Aren't those who serve unknown and search for opportunities for service blessed?

Not only those who are known but also those who remain unknown, create. There is no effort or prayer bigger than the service done by the unknown hands of love. Albrecht Dürer painted a picture of the hands of his friend in prayer. Is it easy to find such beautiful hands? Is it possible to find hands as sacred as those? And can any hands but those have a right to pray? So few hands must have had the good fortune to love and pray as those hands did.

40   Discrimination, with Eyes Fully Open

I was in a big city. Some young men came there to meet me. They started asking, "Do you believe in God?"

I said, "No. What relationship is there between belief and God? I know God."

Then I told them a story...

There was a revolution in some country. The revolutionaries there were busy changing everything. They were determined to destroy religion as well. In this context an old monk was arrested and brought to the court. He was asked, "Why do you believe in God?"

That monk replied, "No gentlemen, I do not believe. But God is there, so what can I do?"

They asked, "How do you know that he exists?"

That old man said, "Ever since my eyes opened I have seen no one but him."

The old man's replies were like putting fuel on a fire. The revolutionaries became very angry and said, "Very soon we will kill all your monks and nuns. What then?"

That old man laughed and said, "As God wishes!"

"But we have decided to destroy all signs of religion. We will not leave any sign of God in the world."

The old man replied, "My son, you have chosen a very difficult job. But as God wills it! How will you destroy every sign? Whatever remains will proclaim his existence. At least you will be there, so you will be proclaiming it. It is impossible to get rid of God because God is all-pervading."

All these misunderstandings have cropped up because God has been compared to man.

God is not a person. He is what he is. And the thought of believing in God has also created a lot of misunderstandings.

What is the meaning of believing in light? It can only be seen when your eyes are open.

Belief is a supporter of ignorance, and ignorance is a sin. What can take a person to the truth is not blind faith, blindfolded eyes, but discriminating with his eyes fully open.

Truth is God. There is no other God except the truth.

41   Truth Is Very Internal

I urge a change of mind from the very roots. No change that happens on the superficial level of the body will be of any real value. Simply changing the way you behave is not enough, because without an inner revolution you will only be deceiving yourself.

But even the people in whom the idea of changing the self arises, very soon become preoccupied with changing their clothes but not their hearts. This is the ultimate way of deceiving yourself. It is absolutely necessary to beware of it; otherwise even renunciation will still only happen externally. The world is on the outside but if even renunciation is also external then your life will be lost on very dark paths.

There is no doubt that the path of desire is one of ignorance. But if renunciation is also something outer it, too, will take you on paths which are strewn with ignorance.

The truth is that ignorance and darkness are the result of your consciousness focusing outside yourself. And it makes no difference whether the object of your outward focus is the world or sannyas. If the mind is engaged with the outer, then whether you are indulging or renouncing your focus will stay out.

If the mind is free from the outer then it will spontaneously come back to the self.

The fallacious notion that the outer will bear fruit is the world.
The realization that the outer is futile is sannyas.
I have heard a story...

In a city two deaths occurred on the same day. It was a very strange coincidence. One person who died was a yogi and the other was a prostitute, and both left this world on the same day and at the same moment. They lived in houses that were opposite each other. They both lived at the same time and died at the same time.

This coincidence surprised everyone in the city, but there was a deeper surprise to come, which was not known to anyone except the yogi and the prostitute. As soon as they died, messengers of death descended to carry them away. But these messengers carried the prostitute to heaven and the yogi to hell! The yogi said, "My friends, undoubtedly there has been some mistake. Are you carrying the prostitute to heaven and me to hell? What is this injustice? What darkness is this?"

The messengers replied, "No, sir; there is no mistake nor any injustice or darkness. Kindly look down for a moment."

The yogi looked down towards the earth. There, his body was decorated with flowers and it was being carried in a big procession. Thousands of men were carrying his body to the burning *ghats* to the beat of a drum. At the burning *ghats* a pyre of sandalwood had been made ready for him. On the other side of the road, the dead body of the prostitute was lying. There was nobody even to carry it away, and so vultures and dogs were tearing at it and eating it.

On seeing this, the yogi said, "The people on the earth are far more just!"

The messengers replied, "This is happening because the people on earth knew only what was on the outside. Their approach is no deeper than the body. But the real question is not about the body, it is about the mind. In your body you were a sannyasin, but what was in your mind? Didn't your mind always love the prostitute? Wasn't the thought always alive in your mind that the beautiful music and dancing going on in the prostitute's house were very pleasant, and that your life was without pleasure?

"And on the other hand, there was the prostitute. She was constantly thinking how blissful that yogi's life must be. At night, when you were singing devotional songs, she would weep, lost in her feelings. On one hand, your ego was getting puffed up by being a sannyasin, and on the other she was becoming more and more humble from the torture of her sins. You were becoming harsher and harsher because of your so-called knowledge, and she was becoming softer and softer from the knowledge of her ignorance.

"Finally, all that was left was your personality, eaten up by ego, and hers, which was free from it. At the time of death, you had ego and desire inside, but in her mind, there was neither. Her mind was full of the light of godliness, love and prayer."

The truth of life does not live in external coverings, so what is the use in changing what is on the outside?

Truth is very internal, extremely internal.

To discover it one has to work, not at the circumference of personality but at the center of it. Find that center. If it is found, truth will certainly be found because, after all, it is hidden in the self.

Religion is not a change at the circumference; it is a revolution of the inner being.

Religion is not a performance at the circumference; it is hard work at the center.

Religion is hard work on the self. It is from that labor that the "I" is destroyed and the truth is attained.

Ego: The Only Obstacle 42

Ego makes the heart like a stone. It is the death of all that is true, good, and beautiful in life. That is why there is no other obstacle on our way to godliness except the ego. How can a stone-hearted person know love? And where there is no love, how can there be godliness? For love we require a simple and humble heart – simple and full of feeling. However deep the ego is, to that same depth the heart loses its simplicity and feeling.

What is religion? When someone asks me I say: "Religion is simplicity of heart, the feeling-power of the heart."

But what exists today in the name of religion is the manifestation of ego in very subtle and intricate forms. Ego is the root of all violence.

"I am" – this very feeling is violence. Then "I am something" is an even bigger violence. A violent mind cannot find true beauty because violence makes one harsh. Harshness means closing the doors of the self – and how can someone who has closed the doors within himself relate to all?

There was a saint, Hasan. He had been hungry for several days. He was living outside a village. Some of his companions were visiting him.

They were also tired and hungry on account of their long journey. As soon as they had arrived and settled into that broken house, an unknown person brought them a lot of food and fruit and said, "This insignificant offering is for those who practice penance and who have renounced." When he had left, Hasan said to his companions: "Friends, I will have to go to sleep without food even tonight; because when have I practiced penance and how can I be a renouncer? In truth where am I myself?"

"I am not": whoever knows this, knows godliness.
"I am not": whoever can discover this can find godliness.

Ignorance Is Vocal and Knowledge Is Silent   43

This incident occurred at midday. Some people came to me and said, "There is no God and religion is all hypocrisy."

On hearing their words, I started laughing and they asked, "Why do you laugh?"

I said, "Because ignorance is vocal and knowledge is silent. Is it so easy to say anything about the existence or non-existence of God? Aren't all decisions, arising out of the meager knowledge of man, worth laughing at?"

Those who know the limits of their own knowledge don't make such decisive statements but instead feel unable to speak. And it is in such mysterious moments they also transcend their limits. At such a time they know themselves and also the truth, because truth exists in the self, and the self exists in truth. For isn't the drop found in the ocean and the ocean in the drop? Is it right for a drop which doesn't know itself, to want to know the ocean? And if it fails to find it, might it not say that the ocean does not exist? If the drop can know itself it can know the ocean, too.

Thinking about God is meaningless. I ask you: Do you know yourself? Is anyone who doesn't know himself competent to take a decision about the existence or nonexistence of God?"

"Do you know yourself?" On hearing this question those friends started looking at one another. And don't you also start looking at one another when you hear this question? Remember that without knowing the self there is no purpose to life or appreciation of it. I retold those friends a conversation that had taken place in Greece thousands of years ago...

Someone asked an old sage, "Among all the things of the world, which is the biggest?

The sage replied, "The sky, because whatever exists, exists in the sky and the sky itself does not exist in anything;

The person continued, "And what is the best thing?"

The sage replied, "Grace, because everything can be sacrificed for grace but grace cannot be sacrificed for anything."

Then he asked, "And the most mobile?"

"Thought," responded the sage.

And then the man asked, "And what is the easiest to give?"

The sage replied, "Advice."

"And the most difficult?"

"Knowledge of the self," said the sage.

Surely knowing the self seems to be the most difficult because in order to know it, everything else has to be given up. Knowledge of the self is not possible without giving up all your knowledge first.

Ignorance is a barrier to knowing the self.

Knowledge is a barrier to knowing the self.

But there is also another state where there is neither knowledge nor ignorance. It is in this state that knowledge of the self manifests.

I call that very state *samadhi*, meditation.

The Door to Life through the Process of Death 44

What shall I say about religion? Religion is the door to life through the process of death.

One night I was on a boat. The boat was big and there were many friends with me. I asked them: "This river is flowing fast but where to?"

Someone replied, "Towards the ocean."

It is true that all rivers run to the ocean. But by running to the ocean aren't the rivers running to their own deaths? Rivers will, after all, be lost in the ocean. Perhaps it is for this very reason that ponds do not go towards the ocean. Which wise man would like to move closer to his own death? And it is for this same reason that the so-called wise ones do not approach religion. The ocean is to a river what religion is to man. Religion means losing oneself completely in existence. That will be a great death for the ego. So those who want to save themselves from this become pools of ego and save themselves from merging with the ocean of godliness. The inevitable outcome of merging with the ocean is the elimination of the self. But that death is not really a death, because compared to the life which is gained as a result of that merger, the life that we know now seems like death. I am saying this after having died myself.

For real life to begin one has to die to the false life.

To settle in the vast the atom has to disperse.

What is death on one side will become life on the other.

Death of the ego is the birth of the soul. This is not effacement, this is true isness. Those who cannot understand this truth will remain bereft of life.

A lake is not life for a river but its death, even though becoming a lake may appear to be a kind of security to the river. And the ocean is not death for a river, it is its life, even though the ocean appears to have swallowed it up.

One day Radha asked Krishna: "My lord, this flute is always on your lips. I am very jealous of it. This bamboo flute gets so much of the nectar-like touch of your sweet lips that I am dying of jealousy. Why is it so close to you? Why is it so dear to you? Every time I think: I wish I could be the flute of Krishna. And in future lives, I want to be the flute which rests on your lips."

On hearing this Krishna laughed a great deal and said, "My beloved, it is very difficult to be a flute. Perhaps there is nothing more difficult than that. Only one who can completely annihilate himself, can become a flute. This flute is not merely a piece of bamboo; in fact, it is the heart of a lover. It has no tunes of its own. It has made the tunes of the lover its own music. I sing, it sings. If I am silent, it is silent, and, for this reason, my life has become its own life."

I was passing by and unintentionally overheard this conversation between Radha and Krishna. The mystery of music is revealed in the mystery of being a flute. The key to finding the self is in ending the ego.

What is religion? Religion is the door to life through the process of death.

Religion Lives in the Breaths of Life   45

It is not worth considering whether religion is found in philosophizing or not. Religion is only meaningful when it is your very life, not just a thought.

A lot of religion is found in thoughts. But does that religion elevate you? It only drowns. Does anyone ever set out on an ocean voyage in a boat made of thoughts? But people set out into the ocean of truth with a boat only made of thoughts! So is it any surprise if you see them drowning near the shore? Even a boat made out of paper can take you much farther than a boat made of thoughts; even that is a little more realistic. Thoughts are like dreams; they are not to be trusted.

If religion is only found in thoughts then nothing could be more untrue.

When religion lives only in scriptures it is dead.

As long as religion lives only in words it is inactive.

The religion that lives only in sects it is not religion. Religion becomes alive only when it lives in life. Religion is true only if it lives in the breaths of life. And where there is truth there is power, there is activity. Where there is activity there is life.

A prisoner died. A number of people gathered around his dead body. They were not weeping. They were laughing. On seeing this, I also stopped by with the crowd. The prisoner had served several terms in prison, and there was hardly a crime that he had not committed. A major portion of his life had been spent in prison. But that man had had very religious thoughts. In order to protect religion, he always had at least a big staff in his hand, and when he was not actually uttering abuses, he was very proudly chanting "Rama, Rama". He always used to say: "Death is better than disgrace." This was his life's principle. He had written this, along with religious rituals, on a piece of paper that he placed in an amulet and tied to his arm. Not satisfied with just this, when he was finally released from prison he had the words tattooed on both of his arms. "Rama, Rama" was also tattooed on several parts of his body.

His dead body was lying under the morning sun. His arms declared his philosophy of life, but the truth about his life had been demonstrated by how he had actually lived it. Only then could I understand why people around were not weeping, but laughing.

The situation in which man finds himself in the name of religion is exactly the same.

I want to ask you whether it is right to weep or to laugh at this situation?

What Is Life?

What is life?

It is a sacred fire ritual, but only for those who offer themselves for the sake of truth.

What is life?

A precious opportunity, but only for those who can muster up courage, determination, and effort.

What is life?

A challenging blessing, but only for those who accept it and face it.

What is life?

A great struggle, but only for those who gather all their power and fight for victory.

What is life?

A grand awakening, but only for those who fight against their sleep and unconsciousness.

What is life?

A divine song, but only for those who have made themselves an instrument of the divine.

Otherwise, life is nothing but a protracted and slow death.

Life becomes what we make it. Life is not given, it has to be won.

Life is a constant creation of the self by the self. It is not a destiny, it is creation.

After his very long and boring argument a lawyer angrily said to the judge, "Sir, the jury is sleeping!"

The judge replied, "My learned friend; it is you yourself who have put them to sleep. Kindly proceed in a way that helps them stay awake. I have also narrowly escaped sleeping at times."

If life is a sleepy experience then we should understand that we have done something to make it go to sleep. If life is an experience of pain then we should know that we have done something which has made it painful. Life is an echo of oneself. Life is one's own reflection.

Free from the Mind 47

It was a dark night during the rainy season. The sky was laden with clouds, and as the thunder rolled, lighting flashed between them. A young man was trying to find his way with the help of this lightning. Finally, he reached the door of a hut where a very old sage had lived his whole life. The old man had never left his hut to go anywhere, but whenever someone asked him if he had ever seen anything of the world he would reply, "I have seen it. I have seen it very well. Doesn't the world exist in the self?"

I know that old man. He is sitting within me. It is true that he has never left his home. He is there, and the same person has always been there. And I know that young man very well too, because I am also him.

The young man stood on the front steps for some time. Then, with a feeling of trepidation, he slowly tapped on the door. A voice answered from within, "Who is there? What are you searching for?"

That young man replied, "I do not know who I am. But for several years I have been wandering in search of happiness. I am looking for happiness, and that search has brought me to your door."

There was laughter from inside and then the voice said, "How can one who does not even know himself, find happiness? On the search, no pool of darkness can be allowed beneath a lamp. Yet even to know that you do not know yourself means that you know enough, and so I will open the door. But remember, when someone else's door opens, it is not your door."

The door opened. In a flash of lightning the young man saw the fakir standing before him. He had never seen such beauty. The fakir was absolutely naked. In truth, beauty is always naked; clothes are only there to cover ugliness. The young man surrendered himself at the old man's feet. He placed his head on them and asked, "What is happiness? What is happiness?"

On hearing this, the old man started laughing again and said, "My dear, happiness lies in independence. As soon as you are independent there is an overflow of happiness. Forget my feet, forget everybody's feet. You are searching for a happiness that is dependent on someone else. This is foolish. You are searching on the outside. This is a folly. In fact, the fact you are searching is itself a folly. One who exists on the outside can be sought, but how can the one who exists within the self be sought? Give up all searching and look. It has always been present within."

Then that old man took out two pieces of fruit from his bag and said, "I am giving you these two fruits. They are very magical. If you eat the first one you will understand what happiness is, and if you eat the second one, you will be happy. But you can eat only one of them, because as soon as you eat one of them, the other one will disappear. And remember: if you eat the second fruit, you will not understand what happiness is. Now the choice lies with you. Tell me, which one do you choose?"

That young man hesitated for a moment and then said, "I want to know what happiness is first because without knowing that, how can happiness be found?"

That old sage started laughing and said, "I can see why your search has become so long. If you go on in this way you will not find happiness – not just for years but for several lives – because seeking knowledge about what happiness *is*, is not the same as attaining happiness. Knowledge about happiness and the experience of happiness are two polar opposites. Knowledge about happiness is not happiness; on the contrary, it is pain, misery. To know about happiness but not to be happy yourself is what real misery is. For that simple reason man is more miserable than plants, animals, and birds. But ignorance is also not happiness. It is only being unaware about misery. Happiness is found when you go beyond both knowledge and ignorance. Ignorance is being unconscious of misery. Knowledge is being conscious of it. Happiness is being freed from both knowledge and ignorance.

"The outcome of going beyond both knowledge and ignorance is freedom from the mind itself – and as soon as a person is free from the mind, he reverts to the self. Being rooted in the self is happiness, bliss. It is freedom and it is godliness."

48   Clothes Can Deceive

A friend became a traditional sannyasin. Today was the first time he had come to see me since becoming one. Seeing him dressed in saffron I said, "I was thinking that you had really become a sannyasin – but what is this? Why have you changed the color of your clothes?"

He smiled at my ignorance and said, "A sannyasin has his own dress code."

On hearing this I started to reflect. He asked, "What is there to think about?"

I said, "It is a matter for deep thought because a sannyasin should have no special dress code, and if he does then he is not a sannyasin."

Perhaps he did not understand what I was saying because he asked, "After all, a sannyasin must wear something – or do you want him to go around naked?"

I replied, "There is no ban on wearing clothes and there is no condition that one should not wear them. The question is about insisting on wearing something particular or on wearing nothing. My friend, this code is not about clothes but about insistence."

He said, "But wearing special clothes keeps reminding me that I am a sannyasin."

Now it was my turn to laugh. I said, "What one is doesn't have to be remembered. Remembering what one is *not* is what needs nurturing. Is a spirituality which we can only remember because of our clothes any spirituality at all? Clothes are very superficial and shallow. Even skin is not deep enough. Flesh and marrow are also not very deep – neither is the mind. Except for the soul, there is nothing deep enough to become the abode of spirituality. And remember, those whose focus is fixed on the superficial will not experience the inner. Those whose attention is on clothes cannot have any awareness of their soul – for that very reason. What else is the world but the mind focused on outer garments? One who can free himself from clothes is a sannyasin."

Then I told him a story…

An impersonator went to a king's palace and said, "I want five rupees as a donation."

The king said, "I can give a performing artist a reward but not a donation."

The impersonator smiled and went away. But as he was leaving he said, "Oh king: I will accept the reward only if I am also offered the donation. Kindly remember this."

The incident passed. After some days the news that a wonderful sannyasin had arrived spread like an electric current throughout the capital. Outside the city a young sannyasin was sitting in deep meditation. He would not speak, he would not open his eyes, and he would not move. Larger and larger crowds came to look at him. Flowers, fresh fruit, dried fruit, and sweets were piling up beside him, but he was in deep meditation and so knew nothing about them.

One day passed, another day passed, and the crowd kept getting bigger. On the morning of the third day, the king himself went to see the sannyasin. He offered one hundred thousand gold coins at the sannyasin's feet and prayed for his blessings, but the sannyasin was as still as a rock. Nothing was able to tempt or move him. So even the king had failed. As he was returning to his palace the crowd were still shouting "Hail, hail!" to the sannyasin.

But on the fourth day the people saw that the saint had disappeared during the night. On that very day the impersonator reappeared at the king's court and said to him, "Now you have offered me a donation of one hundred thousand gold coins kindly give me my reward of five rupees."

The king was amazed. He said to the man, "You fool, why did you ignore those one hundred thousand gold coins? And now you are asking for five rupees!"

The impersonator replied, "Oh king; as you wouldn't give me a donation, how could I accept one the second time? Isn't it enough to get a reward for one's work? And what is more, when I was being a sannyasin, even if I was a fake one I was still a sannyasin and so I had to maintain the dignity of sannyas."

If you think over this story, a number of things will strike you. Impersonators can be sannyasins. Why? – because within a so-called sannyasin's clothes there is room for an impersonator to hide. Wherever a garment has some significance it provides opportunities for impersonation.

That impersonator was actually of a saintly disposition, and that is why when he was offered a hundred thousand gold coins he was willing to accept only five rupees. But it would not be right to expect all impersonators to be so saintly. The king was deceived by his clothes.

Because dress codes can deceive people deceivers and cheats have made them very important. And when a person succeeds in deceiving others, that success becomes a strong foundation for deceiving himself.

They say, *satyameva jayate*, only truth triumphs. This is a very dangerous yardstick because then people get the idea that whoever triumphs is authentic. If "truth succeeds" then it doesn't take long for the mind to reach the conclusion that whosoever succeeds must be true.

A spirituality which can be impersonated is not real spirituality – because then there will be nothing easier for an impersonator to imitate. If impersonators can be sannaysins, then sannyasins can also be impersonators.

The fact is that there is no dress code for sannyasins. There can only be dress codes for impersonators. And if there is no dress code for sannyasins, then the very question of protecting their dignity does not arise. That concern belongs to the impersonators, not to the sannyasins. And such concern will only be found in the impersonator who knows himself to be just a mimic.

Those who have started thinking of themselves as sannyasins on the basis of their outer garments are just Ramas in a Rama–Leela play who start taking themselves to be Rama.

I know one such Rama. After playing the Rama once in a play, he has never cast off the role. People say he is mad.

Impersonators can dress up as sannyasins, but when they also start believing themselves to be sannyasins they are not only mimics, they have gone insane too.

49   Happy as a King

An emperor was up to his neck in worries. When worries drown you, they do so totally – because once one worry has found its way in, others follow by the same route. Whosoever allows one worry to enter unconsciously opens the door for many. For this very reason worries always arrive as crowds! No one ever faces just one worry.

It seems surprising that emperors are often drowning in worries – although, the truth is that only one who has become free from all worries is an emperor. The slavery of worry is so enormous that even the total power of an emperor fails to wash it away. Perhaps for this very reason the power of empires also ends up in the service of worries.

A man wants to be an emperor for the power and independence it brings. But in the end, he finds that nobody is more powerless, dependent, and unsuccessful than an emperor, because a person who wants to enslave others, ultimately becomes the slave of slaves himself. Whatever we want to bind, ultimately succeeds in binding us. For independence, not only freedom from the slavery of others, but even freedom from the mentality of wanting to enslave others is essential.

This emperor was similarly enslaved. He had started out trying to conquer the heavens, but after all his victories he came to realize that he was seated on the throne of hell. Whatever is won through the ego ultimately proves to be a hell – and the ego can never gain heaven because in heaven there is no ego. Now he wanted to be free from his self-won hell. But it is difficult to attain heaven and easy to lose it whereas it is easy to reach hell and difficult to lose it.

He wanted to be free from the fire of worry. Who wouldn't like to be? Who would want to remain sitting on the throne of hell? But whoever wants to sit on a throne will have to sit on the throne of hell. Remember, there is no throne in heaven. It is just that the thrones of hell look like the thrones of heaven from a distance.

Day and night, sleeping or awake, that emperor was struggling with his worries. But with one hand a person gets rid of his worries and with a thousand hands he invites more in. The emperor wanted to be free from all worries but he also wanted to become a great monarch. Perhaps he thought that once he became a worldwide sovereign he would get rid of all his worries. The folly of man keeps coming to such conclusions. That is why he was looking for new areas to rule every day. Each evening the setting sun should not find his kingdom's boundaries in the same place that the rising sun had found them in the morning. He dreamed of silver and breathed in gold. In life, such dreams and such breaths are very dangerous because the dreams of silver become chains for your breaths, and the breaths of gold pour poison into your soul. The stupor that results from the wine of ambition can only be broken by death.

The noontide of the emperor's life was over. He was reaching the far end of the day: death had started sending its intimations.

Every day his strength was decreasing and his worries were increasing. His life was in turmoil. What a man sows in youth he harvests in old age. Poisonous seeds do not trouble you at the time they are sowed, they only trouble you when the harvest is reaped. Those who can see such misery in a seed do not sow it. You cannot get rid of a seed once it has been sown; it will have to be harvested, there is no escape from that.

The emperor stood in the midst of the harvest that he himself had sown. He even thought of committing suicide in order to escape from it. But the greed for being an emperor and the hope of being a universal monarch in the future would not allow him even that. He could lose his life – he had actually already lost it – but it was beyond his power to give up being an emperor. That desire was his very life, and only such desires – which look like life – destroy it.

One day, trying to get rid of his worries, he went to the green foothills. But it is more difficult to run away from one's worries than to run away even from one's funeral pyre. A person may be able to run away from his funeral pyre, but not from his worries because the funeral pyre is on the outside, and the worries are inside. Whatever is inside you will always be with you. Wherever you are, it will be there. Without changing the self from the very roots, there will be no escape from it.

The emperor was riding along in the forest. Suddenly he heard the sound of a flute. There was something in that sound that made him stop abruptly and turn his horse towards the music.

Near a hilly waterfall, under the shade of a tree, a young shepherd was playing on his flute and dancing. His sheep were resting nearby. The monarch said to him, "You appear to be as happy as if you have found a kingdom."

The young man replied, "Please, I pray that existence does not give me a kingdom. In this moment I am an emperor, but no one who gains a kingdom remains an emperor."

The king was surprised and asked, "Tell me what you possess that makes you an emperor."

The young man replied, "It is not through wealth but through independence that a person becomes an emperor. I have nothing except myself. I have myself with me and there is no wealth bigger than that.

I cannot think of anything an emperor has which I don't have. I have eyes that can see beauty, I have a heart that loves, and I have the ability to enter into prayer. The light that the sun gives to me is not less than the light it gives to an emperor, and the light that the moon showers on me is not less than the light it showers on an emperor. Beautiful flowers blossom as much for me as for him. An emperor eats his fill and clothes his body; I do the same.

"So what does an emperor have that I don't? Perhaps the worries of a monarch – but may God save me from them! A funeral pyre is better than worries. There are, on the other hand, many other things that I have which an emperor doesn't: my independence, my soul, my happiness, my dance, my music. I am happy with what I am, and therefore I am an emperor."

The emperor heard the views of the young man and said, "My dear young man, what you say is right. Go and tell everybody in the village that the emperor also says the same thing."

50   Unasked Opinions

One morning I had just got up when a few people came to see me. They said, "Some people are criticizing you very much. One says you are an atheist, another says you are irreligious. Why don't you contradict all these useless remarks?"

I replied, "Whatever is useless does not call for a reply. Don't we only make something important when we accept it as worthy of being contradicted?"

On hearing this, one of them said, "But it is not right to allow wrong things to prevail in the world."

I replied, "You are right. But those who need to criticize and indulge in rumors can never be stopped. They are big inventors and will always find new ways. I will tell you a story concerning this."

And the story that I told them, I shall repeat for you...

It was a full-moon night and the whole earth was drowning in bright moonlight. Shankar and Parvati, seated on their beloved bullock, Nandi, set off on a little ride. But no sooner had they gone a few paces than some people met them on the way. Seeing them on Nandi's back, the people said, "Look at that shameless pair! Both of them are seated on that poor bullock – as if it had no life." On hearing these remarks, Parvati got down and started walking.

But only a little distance ahead they met some other people who said, "Oh how interesting! Who is this man who rides on the back of the bullock – making a delicate creature go on foot? There should be a limit to such shamelessness." On hearing this, Shankar dismounted and put Parvati back on Nandi's back.

They had hardly gone a few steps further when some other people said, "What a shameless woman she is! She is making her husband walk while she sits on the bullock! My friends, the Kaliyug, the end of the world, has begun." On hearing this, both of them started going on foot by Nandi's side.

They had moved forward only a few steps when some other people said, "Look at those fools! They have such a strong bullock with them and yet they are still going by foot."

Now, they were in great difficulty. There was nothing left for Shankar and Parvati to do. They stopped with Nandi under a tree to address the problem. Until then, Nandi had been silent. Now he laughed and said, "Shall I tell you a solution? Both of you should put me on your heads!"

As soon as they heard this, Shankar and Parvati came to their senses, and they both got up onto Nandi's back again. Even then, people passing by kept saying things. In fact, how can people pass by without saying something? But now Shankar and Parvati were enjoying their journey in the moonlight and were oblivious of all the people passing by.

In life, if you want to reach somewhere then it is suicidal to heed the words of everybody who meets you on the way.

In fact, a person whose opinion has any value will never express it without being asked.

Also remember that the movement of a person who does not act according to his own insight and intelligence becomes like the movement of dry leaves flying in the force of the wind.

Life and Death Are Not Separate 　　51

A person went to Confucius and said, "I am very tired. Now I want to rest. Is there any way?"

Confucius told him, "Life and rest are two contradictory words. If you want to live do not ask for rest. Rest is death."

The person's forehead wrinkled with worry and he asked, "Then shall I never find rest?"

Confucius replied, "You will find it; you will definitely find it," and pointing to the graveyard in front of them, he said, "Look at those graves. There is peace in them. There is rest in them."

I do not agree with Confucius. Life and death are not separate. They are like the moving breaths of existence. Neither is life merely action nor death merely rest. In fact, one who is not at rest during life cannot be at peace even after death. Doesn't restlessness during the day make your sleep at night restless too? Won't echoes of the restlessness of your whole life torture you after death? Death will follow the same pattern that your life has followed; it is not the opposite of life, it is complementary to it.

It is right that you should not be inactive during your life because that is tantamount to being dead when you are alive, but life becoming all action is not right either. That, too, is not life. That is idiocy – an idiotic mechanization.

Life will be perfectly fruitful only if there is action on the circumference and inaction at the center: action on the outside, peace within; movement on the outside, calm within. A complete person is born only when a personality full of action is joined with a peaceful soul. The life of such an individual is peaceful, and his death will be an ultimate liberation.

The Priest and the Sudra 52

I went to a meeting. It was a meeting of sudras, untouchables. The very conception of the sudra fills my heart with tears. On reaching the meeting I felt very unhappy and sad. What has man done to man? The people who are building insurmountable walls between one person and the next are called religious! What greater downfall could religion have than this? And if this is religion, then what is irreligion? It seems that the dens of irreligion have stolen the banners of religion, and the scriptures of Satan have become the scriptures of God.

True religion is not separation, it is oneness. It is not duality, it is non-duality. It is not found by building walls but by demolishing them. But the so-called religions have only been creating divisions and erecting walls. They have used their power to fragment and divide man. Surely this has not been done without a reason? The fact is that there can be neither organizations nor exploitation without dividing man against man. If mankind is one and equal, then the very basis of exploitation will be destroyed, because for exploitation to occur, inequality, sects, and caste systems are essential. For this very reason, religions, in many forms, have supported inequality, sects, and castes. A society without sects and castes is automatically against exploitation. To accept the equality of all people is to discard exploitation.

So if no divisions are made between one person and the next there can be no organizations and religious sects. Division creates fear, envy, and hatred, and finally enmity. Enmity gives birth to organizations. Organizations are born out of enmity and not out of friendship. Hatred, not love, is their foundation stone.

Organizations are formed out of a fear of enmity. Organizations become powerful. Power makes exploitation and fulfilling one's lust for authority easier. As power expands it develops into a lust to rule.

In this way, religion secretly turns into politics. Religion moves in front and politics follows behind. Religion ends up being just the cover and politics becomes the driving force behind. In fact, wherever there are organizations and sects, there is no religion there; there is only politics. Religion is a search through meditation, it is not organization. In the name of different religious organizations, different politics keep on making their moves. Yes, in the absence of organizations there can be *religion*, but not religions with their worshippers, priests, and the like.

God has been turned into a profession. Vested interests have even attached themselves to God. What can be more obscene and irreligious than that? But the power of propaganda is boundless and with constant propaganda even absolute lies will become truths. So what wonder is it that the worshippers and priests – who are themselves in the business of exploitation – become supporters of the systems of exploitation? Religions have served as strong pillars for systems of social exploitation. Having woven a net of imaginary doctrines, they have portrayed the exploiters as religious people and the exploited as sinners. The ones being exploited have been told that their suffering is the result of their bad deeds in their past lives. In truth, religions have given a lot of opium to the people!

An old sudra asked me at the end of the meeting: "Can I go to the temples?"

I said, "To the temples? But what for? God himself never visits these temples that belong to the priests."

God has no other temple but existence. All the other temples and mosques are an invention of the priests. There is not even a distant relationship between these temples and God. God and the priests have never been on talking terms! Temples are the creation of the priests, and the priests are the creation of Satan. They are the disciples of Satan. The scriptures and religious sects are responsible for man being pitted against man. They have talked of love, but have spread the poison of hatred – in fact it is easier to administer poison when it is cloaked in sugar-coated pills. But even then, people have not been wary of the priests – whenever they think about God, they get involved with the priests. And this is the fundamental cause of mankind's weakening connection with God. All the time the priests have been busy murdering God. Apart from them, God has no other murderer.

If you want to choose God you cannot choose the priest. Both cannot be worshipped at the same time. As soon as a priest enters a temple, God leaves! In order to establish a relationship with God, it is necessary to get rid of the priests. They are the only obstacle between a devotee and God. Love does not tolerate anyone in between, nor does prayer.

It was early in the morning. It was still dark. As soon as the door of a temple opened, a sudra climbed up the steps to the door. He was about to step through the doorway when the priest shouted out in anger, "Stop, stop, you sinner! If you go one step further you will be completely destroyed. You have polluted the sacred steps of the temple of God."

The frightened sudra stepped back. Tears came into his eyes as if someone had stabbed his heart which was thirsty for God. He wept and said, "Oh, God, what is this sin of mine which means I cannot see you?"

The priest said – on God's behalf – "You have been impure since your birth. You are a storehouse of sins."

The sudra prayed, "Then I will practice spiritual disciplines to purify myself. I do not want to die without seeing God."

Then for years that sudra could not be found. No one knew where he had gone. People had almost forgotten about him when, suddenly, he came back to the village one day. The temple was situated near the entrance of the village. The priest saw the sudra walking beside the temple. There was a new luster on his face. There was a hitherto unknown peace in his eyes. Even around his face there was a halo of light. But he did not even lift his eyes towards the temple. He looked absolutely indifferent and disinterested by it.

The priest could not control himself. He called out to him and asked, "Hello! Is your attempt at self-purification over?"

At this the sudra laughed and moved his head in assent.

The priest asked him, "Then why don't you come into the temple?"

The sudra replied, "Sir, what would I do if I come in? When God appeared before me, he said, 'Why did you go looking for me at the temple? There is nothing there. I myself have never been to those temples, and even if I were to go, do you think the priest would allow me to enter?'"

Religion Cannot Be Purchased 53

A multimillionaire I know built several temples. He has invested his money in religion and has great expectations. He is a very shrewd businessman and is in the habit of making a tenfold profit.

Even in the business of religion he does not want to lag behind anyone. The fact is that he is not in the habit of lagging behind. If he doesn't lag behind where money is concerned why should he do so with religion? In matters of the world, he is in front of and on top of others – and now he has even made provision for the other world! Heaven is now a certainty and he is, therefore, without a care in the world.

Not only this earth, but even heaven can be purchased with money. That is why money is so important. Money is even higher than religion, because money cannot be purchased with religion, but religion can certainly be purchased with money. When money can buy you religion, the fear of accumulating your money through foul means also disappears, because without foul means money cannot be accumulated. Wealth is basically theft. Wealth is exploited blood. But in the Ganges of religion, all sins are washed away, and the Ganges of religion starts flowing wherever a Bhagirath – the king whose rigorous efforts brought the Ganges down to earth – of wealth beckons. In this way, religion becomes the basis of irreligion.

But how can religion become the basis of irreligion? Surely, such religion is not true religion?

What can be purchased with wealth is not religion.

I have heard...

One morning a rich man knocked at the gates of heaven. Chitragupta, the doorkeeper of heaven, asked, "Brother, who is there?"

"Me! Don't you know me? Hasn't the news of my death reached here yet?"

Chitragupta asked, "What do you want?"

The rich man said in anger, "Is that something to be asked? I want to enter heaven;" and so saying he pulled a bundle of money from his coat and offered it to Chitragupta.

At this Chitragupta laughed loudly and said, "My brother, the customs of your world cannot work here, nor are these coins in circulation. Kindly keep your money to yourself."

At this, the rich man started to behave like someone poor and meek. The power which had given him strength in the past was proving to have absolutely no substance there.

Chitragupta asked him, "What have you done to deserve entry into heaven?"

After lot of thought the rich man said, "I gave ten paisa as a gift to an old woman."

Chitragupta immediately asked his co-worker: "Is this true?"

The co-worker looked into the files and said, "Yes sir. It is true."

Chitragupta asked the rich man, "What else have you done?"

The rich man thought again and said, "I gave five paisa to an orphan."

The co-worker searched among his papers and found that this fact was also true.

Chitragupta asked, "Anything else?"

The rich man said, "That is all. I can remember only those two things."

Chitragupta asked his co-worker: "What should be done?"

The co-worker said, "The fifteen paisa can be returned to him and he can be sent to hell. Fifteen paisa for heaven is too cheap."

But can heaven be reached by giving more money? A paisa is, after all, a paisa – even if you put one on top of the other and make the pile higher, a paisa will always be a paisa.

In fact, religion cannot be purchased in any way – neither for less money, nor for more – because money does not circulate in the world of religion. Religion cannot be purchased even by renouncing your wealth, because trying to buy heaven by renouncing your wealth is the same as trying to buy it *with* your wealth. Money has no value as far as religious values are concerned. The very language of money is irrelevant for religion.

The reality of one's self cannot be purchased. The reality of one's self is religion, the reality of one's self is heaven – and it is not found outside the self. It is always present within the self. You do not have to go into religion, you simply have to wake up and know that you have been in religion all along. Just as a fish lives in the sea, so we dwell in religion. But even when the fish is in the sea, it can still leave the sea in its sleep, in its dreams. Our condition is the same: when we are in the world we are dreaming. Both indulgence and renunciation are dreams. Both palaces and temples are dreams.

Neither the palaces nor the temples that are built in dreams can bring awakening. The path to awakening is different. It is found when we move our consciousness from the seen to the seer. Our sleep is as deep as the attention we give to the seen, and awakening comes closer as our attention moves back to the seer. When our attention returns totally to the seer, the seen and the seer all disappear, and the totality that remains is religion. This is truth. This is ultimate freedom.

The First Step of the Ladder   54

What is the first truth in the search for ultimate truth? The first truth is for an individual to know himself for what he is, as he is. This is the first step of the ladder. But on most ladders this first step is missing, and so they are only ladders in name and cannot be used for climbing. If someone wants, he can carry such a ladder on his shoulders, but it will be impossible to climb it.

Man deceives others, deceives himself, and wants to deceive even God. In these attempts he loses himself. He has created all the smoke that blinds his eyes.

Aren't our civilization, our culture and our religions beautiful names for similar deceptions? Haven't we made a vain attempt to cover up our lack of civilization, culture, and religion behind this smoke? And what has the result been? The result has been that on account of these very civilizations we have not been able to become civilized, and because of our religions we have not been able to become religious – because untruth can never become the way that leads to truth.

Truth itself is the door to truth. Only after giving up all self-deceptions can the way to truth become clear and unobstructed. It is essential to remember that ultimately you cannot deceive yourself. This day or the next the deceptions will crack and the truths will be revealed. For this very reason, self-deception ultimately turns into remorse. But repentance cannot do what being aware in advance can.

Why do we want to deceive? Doesn't fear exist behind all our deceptions? But is the root cause of fear destroyed by deception? On the contrary, with deception, such roots get buried and grow deeper. In this way they do not die; they become more alive and more powerful. For this very reason, still bigger deceptions have to be invented to cover and hide them, and then an endless chain of deceptions begins in which cowardice goes on increasing and man becomes a sad, small heap of meekness and cowardliness. Then he starts fearing himself as well – and this fear becomes a hell.

In life, it is not right to hide behind deceptions out of fear. What is right is to search out the root cause of fear. You should not suppress fear; you should uncover it. Ultimate liberation is impossible if there is suppressed fear. Only after knowing this fear, after uncovering it, can you become free from fear.

For this very reason, I consider courage to be the greatest religious quality. In the temple of life there is no entry through the back door. Existence only welcomes the one who struggles on courageously.

In a big city in England, one of Shakespeare's plays was being performed. This happened some years ago when it was considered sinful for a gentleman to watch a play, and the question of a priests seeing one did not even arise. Religion is, after all, their sole domain! But one priest was finding it impossible to avoid the temptation of seeing the play. He tried in the same way that we often do in life. He wrote to the manager of the theater and asked, "Can you arrange for me to enter through the back door of the theater so that no one will see me?"

The manager sent his reply: "I am sorry. There is no door here which is not seen by God."

I also want to say the same to you. There is no back door through which you can enter the truth. God is standing at all the doors.

55   Who Is Minding the Shop?

This is a story about a journey. Some old men and women were going on a pilgrimage. A saint was also with them. I was listening to them talking. The saint was explaining to the party, "What happens after life depends on how a man was thinking at the end of his life. One who has taken care of the end of his life has taken care of everything. God must be remembered at the time of death. There have been sinners who remembered the name of God by mistake at the time of their death and they are enjoying the pleasures of heaven today."

The saint's talk was producing the desired effect. Those old people were going on a pilgrimage in their last moments and their hearts were elated to hear what they wanted to: "Really the question is not about life, but about death. To get rid of the sins of a lifetime it is enough to remember the name of God, even by mistake." In their case, it was not even by mistake but because they had decided that they were going on this pilgrimage. Naturally they were happy, and out of this happiness they were also taking good care of the saint.

I was sitting just in front of them. On hearing the saint, I laughed, and the saint asked me in anger, "Don't you believe in religion?"

I said, "Where is religion? Only the coins of irreligion are circulating here, disguised as religion – and it is only bad coins that demand faith. Where anyone's discriminating intelligence will not be in their favor, faith is demanded. Faith murders discretion. But neither are blind men ready to accept that they are blind, nor are the faithful ready to admit that they are blind followers.

"The conspiracy committed by the blind and their exploiters has nearly cut the very roots of religion. There is the show of religion and the practice of irreligion. Have you ever thought about what you have been telling these old people? 'Whatever their lives have been like, their thoughts must be pure at the end.' Can there be anything more dishonest than this? Is it possible? If the seed is a neem seed, then the tree will be a neem tree – and you want to pick a mango! Only the essence of the life that has passed can appear before the consciousness at the time of death. What is death? Isn't it the fulfillment of life itself? How can it be in opposition to life? It is only an extension of it. It is only the fruit of life.

"All imaginary thoughts – like the story of the sinner Ajamil who at the time of his death called for his son Narayan, and because he uttered the name of God unintentionally, he became free from all his sins and attained ultimate liberation – will not work. What inventions will the sinning mind of man not make? And there will always be a person to exploit these terrified people. Is there really a name for God? Remembrance of God is an inner state of feeling. The state of feeling in which the ego is eliminated is the right state for remembering God. Only one who keeps shaking off the dust of the ego throughout his life can ultimately find the clear mirror of egolessness. This cannot happen by simply uttering some name by mistake.

"If someone who mistakenly believes a name to be God's name goes on living with this misapprehension his whole life, his consciousness will only be filled with more unconsciousness rather than divine consciousness. The mere repetition of a word does not awaken consciousness; it puts it to sleep. We do not know why Ajamil was calling his son Narayan. The most likely explanation is that finding he was at the end of his life, he wanted to explain some unfinished business to his son.

"In the last moments, only the essence of your whole life appears, and can appear, before your consciousness."

Then I narrated an incident to them...

An old shopkeeper lay on his deathbed. Around his bed sat the members of his family, all in sorrow. The old man suddenly opened his eyes and asked with great anxiety. "Is my wife here?"

His wife said, "Yes. I am here."

"And my oldest son?"

"He also."

"And the remaining five boys?"

"They too."

"And my four daughters?

"They are also here. You need not worry. Please lie down and rest," his wife said.

"What do you mean?" asked the dying man, trying to sit up, "then who is minding the shop?"

Where Is Happiness?   56

You are asking "Where is happiness?"
I will tell you a story. That story contains the answer.

One day the people of this world had just woken from their sleep when they heard a strange announcement. Such an announcement had never been heard before. Nobody understood where this unprecedented announcement was coming from, but its words were very clear. Perhaps they were coming from the sky, or it maybe they were coming from within. No one knew their source.

"Oh, people of the world! There is a free gift of happiness from God, a guaranteed opportunity to get rid of all your troubles. At midnight today, whoever wants to get rid of his troubles should gather them into an imaginary bundle and throw them away outside the village. Before returning, he should gather whatever happiness he desires into that same sack and return home before sunrise. In place of his troubles he will have happiness. Whoever fails to take advantage of this opportunity will fail forever. This opportunity has come now because the wish-fulfilling tree has descended onto this earth for just one night. Have faith and gather its fruit. Trust will bear fruit."

EARTHEN LAMPS

This announcement kept being repeated all day until sunset. As the night approached, even the skeptics started believing it. Who could be so foolish as to miss this opportunity? And was there anyone who had no troubles and no desire for happiness? Everyone started bundling up his troubles. Everyone had only one care: that no troubles should be left behind. By the time midnight was approaching, all the houses in the world were empty and countless people with bundles of troubles were moving, like rows of ants, towards the outskirts of their towns. In order to prevent the troubles from coming back, they walked further and further away from their towns to throw them away, and like mad people they all began hastily collecting happiness after midnight.

Everyone was hurrying in case the morning should come while some happiness was still untied in a bundle. There was so much happiness, and the time was so limited. Nevertheless people hurried and somehow reached their homes around sunrise after having gathered it all. On reaching home they stared, unable to believe their eyes. In place of their huts there were tall palaces, kissing the sky. Everything was golden. Happiness was raining down. Whatever they had wanted was available to them.

This was their first surprise, but there was an even bigger one. Even after discovering all of this, people still had no happiness on their faces. Their neighbors' joy was giving them pain. Their old troubles had disappeared, but they had been replaced with entirely new troubles and worries. The troubles had changed, but people's minds were the same and so they were still unhappy. The world had changed, but the people were the same, and, therefore, everything was still the same.

There was, of course, one person who had not accepted the invitation to surrender his pain and collect happiness. He was a naked monk. He had poverty and only poverty, and taking pity on his foolishness everyone had asked him to join them: the king himself was going, so of

166

course the monk should go. But he had laughed and said, "Whatever is on the outside is not happiness. And where can I go in search of that which is within? I have already discovered that after giving up all searching."

People had laughed at his madness and felt sorry for him. They considered him to be an absolute fool. And when all their huts had been converted into palaces and gems were scattered like pebbles and stones in front of their houses, they again said to the monk: "Haven't you realized your mistake even now?"

But the monk laughed again and said, "I was thinking of asking you all the same question."

57   Fear of Death

I was sitting beside an eighty-four-year-old man who was dying. He had every disease that a person could possibly have, and all at the same time. For a long time he had been putting up with intolerable pain. Eventually he had also lost his sight. Occasionally he would faint. He had not got out of bed for several years. His life was pain and only pain. But even in that condition he wanted to live. He was not ready for death even then.

Even though your life may have become worse than hell, no one ever wants to die. Why is this lust for life so blind and unfulfilled? It forces you to put up with so much. What is this fear of death? And how can you be afraid of death when you have not even experienced it? In reality, you can only be afraid of the known. Why be afraid of the unknown? There can only be a desire or quest to know the unknown.

The old man would start weeping in front of whoever came to see him. There was complaint after complaint. Complaints do not die, even at the moment of death. Perhaps they keep people company even after death.

He had become disgusted with all kinds of physicians, but he had not yet given up hope. With the help of some amulet he still hoped to live on.

I found him alone and asked him, "Do you still want to live?"

He was certainly startled. He must have thought that I had asked a very inauspicious question. Then, in great pain, he said, "Now I have only one prayer to God: that he may take me away." But the untruth of what he was saying was written all over his face.

I remembered a story…

There was a woodcutter. He was helpless, poor, unhappy, and old. He could not cut enough wood anymore even to pay for his food. The strength of his life was diminishing every day. There was nobody in the world with whom he was connected.

One day, after cutting wood in the forest, he was tying it up and muttering, "Even death does not come to my rescue and save me from the painful life of this old age." But no sooner had these words popped out than he felt someone standing behind him. Some invisible and very cold hand was on his shoulder. His body and breath trembled. He turned around but could not see anybody. Even so, someone was certainly there; the weight of a cold hand was clearly on his shoulder. Before he could speak, that invisible power spoke. "I am death. Tell me, what shall I do for you?"

That old woodcutter was lost for words. It was wintertime, but his body was sweating profusely. Somehow, he mustered enough courage and asked, "Oh goddess, take pity on this poor man. What do you want with me?"

Death said, "I am here because you remembered me."

The woodcutter collected himself and said, "Forgive me. I was forgetting myself: kindly help me lift this bundle of wood. I called you only for that, and, in future, either I will not call you, or if, by mistake, I do ever call you, you need not come. By God's grace, I am very happy."

The old man was just thinking about this story when somebody came and told him, "A holy man has arrived. There are many stories about his miraculous powers. Shall I bring him to see you?"

A flash of hope lit the old man's face and somehow he pulled himself up, and said, "Where is this holy man? Call him quickly. After all, I am not so very sick. In fact, it is the doctors who are killing me. God wants to save me, and that is why I am here, in spite of them. Who can kill one whom God wants to save?"

Then I took my leave. But I had just reached home when I received the news that the old man was no longer in this world.

The Ego Wants What No One Else Has 58

A multimillionaire was having a palace built. Just as the palace was being completed he started to die. This is what often happens. The person for whom a palace is being built often dies during the process of its construction, before he can live in it. Such people want to build somewhere to live, but instead they are building their tombs.

This was what was happening. The palace had been built, but the builder was close to his end. And the palace was beyond compare.

The ego wants what no one else has, and just for that, man loses his very soul. The ego, which is a non-existent phenomenon, can only experience its existence by becoming the most important. It can experience its existence only by being the first. That palace was incomparable in all respects – in beauty, in design, and in convenience – and so the multimillionaire was in seventh heaven. The whole capital was talking about him. Whoever saw the palace was spellbound.

At last, the king himself came to see it. He also could not believe his eyes. Compared to this palace his own looked inferior. Inside, he felt jealous, but outwardly he praised the palace. The multimillionaire actually misunderstood his jealousy to be praise. Feeling obliged by the king's appreciation he said, "It is all by God's grace." But in his own heart he

EARTHEN LAMPS

knew that it was all because of his own efforts. Bidding farewell to the king, he said to him at the gate, "I have made only one gate to this palace. In this type of palace theft cannot happen. Whether somebody comes in or goes out he will have to go through this one gate."

An old man was standing in the crowd at the gate. Hearing the rich man's words he laughed loudly. The king asked him, "Why are you laughing?"

He said, "I can only whisper the reason in the rich man's ear." Then he went to the master of the house and whispered in his ear: "I only laughed when I heard you praise the single gate to the palace. In this entire palace that is the only defect. Death will enter from that same gate and will take you away. If that gate had not been there, then you would have been all right."

Man constructs palaces out of life too. In all of them the same defect exists. For this reason, no house proves to be a perfect place to live. To all of them, there is at least one entrance and that entrance becomes the door to death.

But isn't it possible to have an abode in life in which there is no door to death? Yes; it is possible. But such a house has no walls. It has doors and more doors, and because there are only doors, the doors remain invisible. Death can only enter through a door. Where there are only doors and more doors such a door does not exist.

The ego creates walls in life. Then, for the entry and exit of the self, it has to make at least one door, and that is the door of death. The house of the ego cannot remain free from death. One door always remains, and that is the door we have been speaking about. If it does not have that one door, then it will die, it will kill itself.

But there is life without the ego. That life is immortal because it has no door for death to come through, and no walls to surround it.

Where there is no ego there is the soul. The soul is unbounded and unending, like the sky, and what is unbounded and unending is immortal.

59   Prayer Is Not Demanding

I was a guest in a small village. Although it was small it had a temple, a mosque, and it also had a church. People were religious and at dawn every day they would all go to their places of worship. Even at night they would only go to sleep after they had visited them again. There were religious festivals day after day.

But the life of the village was similar to the life of many other villages. Religion and life did not seem to touch one another. Life has its ways and religion has others. They were running parallel to one another, and therefore the question of their meeting did not arise. As a result, their religion became lifeless and their lives were without religion.

What was happening in this village is happening all over the world. I went to each of the places of worship for a day or two, and tried to get some insight into the hearts of God's so-called devotees and priests. I searched their eyes, I probed their prayers, I talked to them, I examined their lives. I observed their comings and goings, their ways of living and I went to some of their houses. I asked their neighbors about them. I heard from the devotees of one God about the devotees of another God. I collected information from the priests of one temple about the priests of another temple. I discussed the learned people of one religion with the learned people of another religion. I came to the conclusion that this religious-looking village was absolutely irreligious. There was a facade of religion and a life of irreligion.

The facade of religion is only needed for a life of irreligion. Aren't places of worship only there to hide places of murder?

God's so-called priests had nothing to do with him. They certainly wanted to keep God because he was bringing in money. And God's devotees had no love for him. They were searching for safety from the fears of the world, and they were praying to God to help them to achieve their worldly desires. Those whose lives were about to end wanted reassurance from God about their futures. Everyone there loved only pleasures and enjoyments. Because their love was only for the world, none of their prayers was, in fact, a prayer to God. In their prayers, they were asking for everything except the divine, and, the fact is that as long as a prayer has a demand in it that prayer is not meant for God.

A prayer becomes a real prayer only when it is free from demands. Even when there is a longing for the divine, that prayer is not a real prayer. Prayer is only real when it is completely free from any demand. For sure, such a prayer cannot contain praise. Praise is not prayer; it is flattery. Praise is bribery. It is not only the manifestation of a low mind, it is also an attempt to deceive – and what could be more foolish than trying to deceive in this way? Doing that, man only deceives himself.

My friend, prayer is not a demand. It is love. It is surrender of the self.

Prayer is not praise. It is a very deep state of gratitude: And where there is an intensity of feeling there are no words.

Prayer is not speech, it is silence, it is a dedication to the infinite. Prayer is not words, it is the music of infinity. Such music begins where other music ends.

Prayer is not worship, nor can there be any places of worship. Prayer has nothing to do with the outer world. It has no relationship with others. It is the innermost awakening of the self.

Prayer is not action, it is consciousness. It is not doing, it is being.

Only the birth of love is necessary for prayer. For that, even the concept of God is unnecessary – it is even obstructive. Wherever there is prayer there is God, but wherever there is the *idea* of God, he is unable to be present just because of that very idea.

Truth is one. God is one. But untruths are many, conceptions are many, and therefore, temples are many. For that very reason temples become not doors but walls in any attempt to reach God.

One who has not found the temple of God in love will find God in no other temple.

What is love? Is it an attachment to God? Attachment is not love. Where there is attachment there is exploitation. In attachment, someone else is the object; the subject is the self. In fact, in love, the other does not exist. Relating to another means involving ego, and where there is ego, there is no God.

Love just exists. It is not *for* someone. It is just there. Where love is for someone, there it is delusion; such "love" is an attachment, a desire. When love is just itself, then it is not a desire, it is prayer. Desire is like the rivers which flow towards the ocean; love is like the ocean itself. It does not flow towards anyone. It is simply itself. It has no attraction to anyone; it exists within itself, and like the ocean, it, too, is prayer. Desire is the flow, the pull and the tension. Prayer is a state. Prayer is peaceful within itself.

Love and perfection are drawn to one another without any reason, without being seen, and without being pushed.

I call this kind of love prayer.

In all other cases our prayers are untrue self-deceptions.

A prisoner who had been condemned to be hanged arrived at a prison. Very soon, the entire prison resounded with his prayers to God. Before the day dawned, his worship and prayer would start. His love for God was unbounded. A non-stop stream of tears flowed from his eyes while he was praying. A feeling aroused by separation and created by his love for God, was there, in every word of his chants. He was a devotee of God, and soon, the other prisoners became his devotees. The prison governor and the other officers started showing him respect. His routine of praying to God continued almost throughout the day and night. His lips would utter "Ram, Ram" while he was getting up, sitting down, or moving. The beads of his rosary were forever turning in his hands. Even his shawl had "Ram, Ram" printed on it.

Whenever the prison governor was on an inspection, he found the man busy with his devotions. But one day, when he arrived, he found that although the day was far advanced the prisoner was still sleeping soundly. His shawl bearing "Ram, Ram" and his rosary were lying neglected in a corner. The governor thought that perhaps he was not feeling well. But on asking the other prisoners he came to know that the prisoner's health was fine, but that no one knew why his prayers to God had suddenly stopped since the evening before.

The governor woke the prisoner and asked him, "Dawn has long since passed. Don't you worship and pray in the morning?"

The prisoner replied, "Worship and pray? Why worship and pray now? I received a letter from home only yesterday telling me that the death sentence has been changed to seven years' imprisonment. Whatever I wanted God to do has been done. It is no longer right to bother the poor fellow for nothing."

60   The Weight of the Ego

Who can prevent man from reaching godliness? And who can tie man to the earth?

What is that power which does not allow the river of life to reach the ocean?

I say it is man himself. The weight of his ego does not allow him to rise higher. It is not the earth's gravitation but the stone-like weight of his ego which does not allow him to rise. We are buried beneath our own weight and have become incapable of movement. The earth only has power over the body – its gravity binds it – but the ego has tied even the soul to this earth. Its very weight means the soul is unable, lacks the power, to rise to the heavens. This body is made of earth. It is born out of it and is merged into it. But because of the ego, the soul is deprived of godliness, and so it is unnecessarily compelled to follow the body.

If the soul cannot attain godliness life becomes intolerably painful. Godliness is the soul's only fulfillment. It is its fullest manifestation, and whenever that fulfillment is obstructed there is pain. When the self's potential to become truth is obstructed there is pain, because full manifestation of the self is bliss.

Do you see this? Do you see this lamp? It is a dead lamp made of earth. But the flame in it is immortal. The lamp comes from the earth, but the flame comes from the heavens. What belongs to the earth stays on the earth, but the flame is constantly rising towards the unknown sky. Man's body is similar – it is made of earth – but his soul is not. The soul is not a dead lamp but an immortal flame. But because of the weight of the ego it, too, cannot rise above the earth.

Only those who are, in every respect, not weighed down by ego will progress towards godliness.

I have heard a story...

On a very inaccessible and high mountain, there was a golden temple dedicated to God. The priest of that temple had become old and had announced that the most powerful person in the whole of mankind would be appointed as his successor. There was no greater opportunity than being appointed to this position.

On the appointed day, the powerful candidates started climbing the mountain. Whoever reached the temple first, situated as it was on the top of the mountain, would surely prove himself to be the most power-ful? When they started the climb, each competitor was carrying a stone on his shoulders to indicate his strength. Each one of them was carrying a weight that he thought represented his power. It was a difficult climb that would last for a month. There was the danger that several of the candidates might lose their lives.

Perhaps for this very reason, there was a pull and a challenge. Hun-dreds of people started testing their luck and endurance. As the days passed, several climbers were left behind. Some of them fell into cre-vasses and valleys together with their stones. Others, as a result of sheer effort and exhaustion left this mortal world still clutching their stones. But even so, the tired and withered ones who were still left moved on with irrepressible motivation. Those who still carried on had no time to think about those who had fallen, nor was it within their capacity to do so.

But one day all the climbers were surprised to see that a person, who had been lagging behind them all, was advancing from behind and moving ahead of them with great speed. He carried no stone on his shoulders to show his strength. This lack of any weight must be the reason why he was moving so quickly: he must have thrown his stone away somewhere. They all started laughing at his foolishness – because what was the point of a person reaching the summit if he no longer carried an indication of his strength?

So, when after a difficult and painful climb of several months the climbers finally reached the temple of God, they could not believe their eyes. They saw that this not very strong man, who had thrown away his stone and had reached the temple first, had been made the temple priest.

Before they could complain against this injustice, the old priest welcomed them and said, "Only one who has become free from the weight of his ego is entitled to enter the temple of God. This young man has given proof of an entirely new kind of strength. A stone weight, which represents the ego, is not really strength. And I respectfully ask you all: Who gave you the idea of carrying stones on your shoulders before you started climbing? And when did he do so?"

About Osho

Osho's unique contribution to the understanding of who we are defies categorization. Mystic and scientist, a rebellious spirit whose sole interest is to alert humanity to the urgent need to discover a new way of living. To continue as before is to invite threats to our very survival on this unique and beautiful planet.

His essential point is that only by changing ourselves, one individual at a time, can the outcome of all our "selves" – our societies, our cultures, our beliefs, our world – also change. The doorway to that change is meditation.

Osho the scientist has experimented and scrutinized all the approaches of the past and examined their effects on the modern human being and responded to their shortcomings by creating a new starting point for the hyperactive 21st Century mind: OSHO Active Meditations.

Once the agitation of a modern lifetime has started to settle, "activity" can melt into "passivity," a key starting point of real meditation. To support this next step, Osho has transformed the ancient "art of listening" into a subtle contemporary methodology: the OSHO Talks. Here words become music, the listener discovers who is listening, and the awareness moves from what is being heard to the individual doing the listening. Magically, as silence arises, what needs to be heard is understood directly, free from the distraction of a mind that can only interrupt and interfere with this delicate process.

These thousands of talks cover everything from the individual quest for meaning to the most urgent social and political issues facing society today. Osho's books are not written but are transcribed from audio and video recordings of these extemporaneous talks to international audiences. As he puts it, "So remember: whatever I am saying is not just for you...I am talking also for the future generations."

Osho has been described by *The Sunday Times* in London as one of the "1000 Makers of the 20th Century" and by American author Tom Robbins as "the most dangerous man since Jesus Christ." *Sunday Mid-Day* (India) has selected Osho as one of ten people – along with Gandhi, Nehru and Buddha – who have changed the destiny of India.

About his own work Osho has said that he is helping to create the conditions for the birth of a new kind of human being. He often characterizes this new human being as "Zorba the Buddha" – capable both of enjoying the earthy pleasures of a Zorba the Greek and the silent serenity of a Gautama the Buddha.

Running like a thread through all aspects of Osho's talks and meditations is a vision that encompasses both the timeless wisdom of all ages past and the highest potential of today's (and tomorrow's) science and technology.

Osho is known for his revolutionary contribution to the science of inner transformation, with an approach to meditation that acknowledges the accelerated pace of contemporary life. His unique OSHO Active Meditations™ are designed to first release the accumulated stresses of body and mind, so that it is then easier to take an experience of stillness and thought-free relaxation into daily life.

Two autobiographical works by the author are available:
Autobiography of a Spiritually Incorrect Mystic,
St Martins Press, New York (book and eBook)
Glimpses of a Golden Childhood,
OSHO Media International, Pune, India (book and eBook)

OSHO International Meditation Resort

Each year the Meditation Resort welcomes thousands of people from more than 100 countries. The unique campus provides an opportunity for a direct personal experience of a new way of living – with more awareness, relaxation, celebration and creativity. A great variety of around-the-clock and around-the-year program options are available. Doing nothing and just relaxing is one of them!

All of the programs are based on Osho's vision of "Zorba the Buddha" – a qualitatively new kind of human being who is able *both* to participate creatively in everyday life *and* to relax into silence and meditation.

Location
Located 100 miles southeast of Mumbai in the thriving modern city of Pune, India, the OSHO International Meditation Resort is a holiday destination with a difference. The Meditation Resort is spread over 28 acres of spectacular gardens in a beautiful tree-lined residential area.

OSHO Meditations
A full daily schedule of meditations for every type of person includes both traditional and revolutionary methods, and particularly the OSHO Active Meditations™. The daily meditation program takes place in what must be the world's largest meditation hall, the OSHO Auditorium.

OSHO Multiversity

Individual sessions, courses and workshops cover everything from creative arts to holistic health, personal transformation, relationship and life transition, transforming meditation into a lifestyle for life and work, esoteric sciences, and the "Zen" approach to sports and recreation. The secret of the OSHO Multiversity's success lies in the fact that all its programs are combined with meditation, supporting the understanding that as human beings we are far more than the sum of our parts.

OSHO Basho Spa

The luxurious Basho Spa provides for leisurely open-air swimming surrounded by trees and tropical green. The uniquely styled, spacious Jacuzzi, the saunas, gym, tennis courts…all these are enhanced by their stunningly beautiful setting.

Cuisine

A variety of different eating areas serve delicious Western, Asian and Indian vegetarian food – most of it organically grown especially for the Meditation Resort. Breads and cakes are baked in the resort's own bakery.

Night life

There are many evening events to choose from – dancing being at the top of the list! Other activities include full-moon meditations beneath the stars, variety shows, music performances and meditations for daily life.

Facilities

You can buy all of your basic necessities and toiletries in the Galleria. The Multimedia Gallery sells a large range of OSHO media products.

There is also a bank, a travel agency and a Cyber Café on-campus. For those who enjoy shopping, Pune provides all the options, ranging from traditional and ethnic Indian products to all of the global brand-name stores.

Accommodation

You can choose to stay in the elegant rooms of the OSHO Guesthouse, or for longer stays on campus you can select one of the OSHO Living-In programs. Additionally there is a plentiful variety of nearby hotels and serviced apartments.

www.osho.com/meditationresort
www.osho.com/guesthouse
www.osho.com/livingin

For More Information

www.**OSHO**.com

a comprehensive multi-language website including a magazine, OSHO Books, OSHO Talks in audio and video formats, the OSHO Library text archive in English and Hindi and extensive information about OSHO Meditations. You will also find the program schedule of the OSHO Multiversity and information about the OSHO International Meditation Resort.

http://OSHO.com/AllAboutOSHO
http://OSHO.com/Resort
http://OSHO.com/Shop
http://www.youtube.com/OSHO
http://www.Twitter.com/OSHO
http://www.facebook.com/pages/OSHO.International

To contact OSHO International Foundation:
www.osho.com/oshointernational,
oshointernational@oshointernational.com